S0-BMC-810

# NO ORTHODOXY
## BUT
## THE TRUTH

*Books by Donald G. Dawe*

*Published by The Westminster Press*

NO ORTHODOXY BUT THE TRUTH:
*A Survey of Protestant Theology*

THE FORM OF A SERVANT
*A Historical Analysis of the Kenotic
Motif*

# NO ORTHODOXY BUT THE TRUTH

*A Survey*

*of Protestant Theology*

*by*

DONALD G. DAWE

THE WESTMINSTER PRESS

*Philadelphia*

Copyright © MCMLXIX The Westminster Press

*All rights reserved*—no part of this book may be reproduced in any form without permission in writing from the publisher, except by a reviewer who wishes to quote brief passages in connection with a review in magazine or newspaper.

Scripture quotations from the Revised Standard Version of the Bible are copyright, 1946 and 1952, by the Division of Christian Education of the National Council of Churches, and are used by permission.

STANDARD BOOK NO. 664–20844–4
LIBRARY OF CONGRESS CATALOG CARD NO. 69–10424

Published by The Westminster Press ®
Philadelphia, Pennsylvania

PRINTED IN THE UNITED STATES OF AMERICA

30.09
321n

L.I.F.E. College Library
1100 Glendale Blvd.
Los Angeles, Calif. 90026

*To my wife*
*Nancy Jane*

027971

# PREFACE

This book was written to help provide some historical perspective on the complex task of rethinking Christian faith in the modern world. The unfolding dialogue between Christianity and modern man already has a considerable history which cannot be overlooked in the search for a theology both relevant and authentic. This book is an introduction to this history in the period from the sixteenth through the eighteenth century. The title—No ORTHODOXY BUT THE TRUTH—is a slogan of the deist John Toland. His words caught the spirit of the new theology emerging in his time. It is a theology that seeks for truth in religion as in science, through man's rational and creative powers rather than through conformity with churchly definitions and traditional authorities. My aim in this book is not simply retelling part of the intellectual history of Western Christendom. My aim is also theological. It is an attempt to identify the sources of strength and of weakness in the newly emerging patterns of Christology. In a very real sense, the quandaries of the early modern period are still a very evident part of our theological situation today.

Thanks are due the Eli Lilly Endowment and the Faculty Research Fund of Macalester College for grants that made this study possible. I am also indebted to Mrs. Donald Brown for her help and to my students and colleagues for their challenge and encouragement.

D. G. D.

*Macalester College*

# CONTENTS

*Chapter I*

# THE POINT

# OF BEGINNING

## *Faith for a World Come of Age*

Contemporary theology is animated by a sharp awareness of the gulf that divides modern men from the Christian faith. If the Christian faith is to become a "live option" for men of the space age, contemporary theologians remind us, it must break out of the narrow confines of its intellectual parochialism. Christianity must be able to address men who live out of the consciousness of a "world come of age," rather than to demand shrilly, but pointlessly, that men abandon, in their religious life at least, their modernity. This awareness of the impact of modernity on religious life is a factor that has served as one of the few axioms of contemporary theology uniting Catholic and Protestant, liberal and conservative. Scripture and tradition, councils and creeds, theism and moralism, have all been challenged by contemporary theologians, at one time or another, in the name of "modern man." What is the source of this dominant and durable idea? How, in fact, did the human race become modern? Why do these changes in human self-understanding so deeply and vitally affect Christian faith? Modernity has been said to be the source of everything from "the abolition of man" to the "death of God," but whence its potence? Answers to these queries are not easy to obtain, for the factors that weigh most heavily in

11

our thinking, and emerge from the deepest levels of our consciousness, are the most difficult to describe. We are not dealing
here merely with a set of ideas. Modern man is not simply the
man who holds to a scientific view of the world, as opposed to
his forebears whose tiny closed world was but a caricature of
the infinite universe in which we dwell. World view, as the more
or less specific awareness of the structures of the world revealed by science, is certainly a vital ingredient in the life of
modern man. Yet there is something even more pervasive. It is
a new form of consciousness or self-awareness. Modern man
is aware of his power to shape his destiny and control his world
to a measure unknown to ancient man. This newfound confidence has freed life increasingly from overt religious control.
The religious vision is no longer the dominant one. Instead of
forcing other modes of self-understanding into conformity with
itself, Christian faith had to relate itself to the new intellectual
vitalities. Such has been the course of the secularization of
Christendom. Not only has it raised deep questions about the intellectual formulations of Christian faith; it has forced upon us
the question of the possibility of Christian faith at all.

Contemporary theology suffers from a kind of historical
myopia in thinking about its problems. The rise of modern man
and his impact upon religion tends to be viewed often as a specifically present-day happening. Although new dimensions are
being added to modernity by ever-accelerating scientific discovery and technological accomplishment, the search for faith
for a humanity come of age is by no means new. As early as the
Renaissance humanists, the first intimations of an autonomous
modern man appeared on the spiritual horizons of the Western
world. With the Enlightenment came the first full realization of
a humanity living out of the strength of its own powers, seeking
to guide its life and interpret its world, not from religious traditions, but from rational power. By the end of the eighteenth
century the world view of Newtonian physics and astronomy,
the historical relativities of Scripture and creed, the place of
myth and symbol in religious thought, and the newfound confidence of man had been felt with revolutionary force in theology. This book is a study of the impact of the rise of the

modern world on theology during the period from the sixteenth through the eighteenth century. To embrace such a movement in one book or by one set of intellectual structures is not a possibility. The aim is not encyclopedic completeness. Even in a work as formidable and profound as Emanuel Hirsch's massive five-volume study of theology from the middle of the seventeenth to the middle of the nineteenth century, the outcome tends to be a cataloging of positions. The crucial questions of meaning and direction are largely left unanswered, save by indirection. My approach to the theology of this period is by means of limitation to one theme. First, I have sought to work from the perspective of a theme that is both central to the theologians considered and integrative of the concerns of the era. This theme is the modernization of Christology. It enfolds in itself the great questions of God and man, revelation and history. Secondly, I have limited the period under consideration to what I call the early modern period, the sixteenth through the end of the eighteenth century. This period has an inner intellectual integration that uniquely suits it to presentation as a kind of case study in the growth of modern religious thought. Like all such limitations of time in historical analysis, this one is not completely closed. It will be necessary to venture into the nineteenth century to round off some loose ends and to provide commentary on the vast and tumultuous issues cast into the hands of later theologians by the work of Hume, Reimarus, and Kant.

Intellectual history cannot be understood as the simple linear advance of new ideas. Rather, there is a rich interplay of action and reaction. This is particularly true in this early modern period when communication of new ideas was frequently inhibited by censor and police, or, at least, discouraged as impiety or heresy. Early Unitarianism, for example, led a kind of underground existence, appearing in differing forms from the sixteenth century onward. Yet it was not until the end of the eighteenth century that it emerged as a continuing church fellowship with a clearly defined, public theology. The same can also be said about deism, which had a way of being rediscovered several times to the recurring delight of its devotees and the dismay of its opponents. This leaves the problem of putting ideas in proper chronological order. Inasmuch as this is a study in intellectual history, not social or institutional history, I have given attention to early beginnings rather than to the later and better known expressions of an idea. What is undertaken here is a case study in the modernization of Christian thought through the unfolding of the new Christology of Protestantism from Socinus to Kant.

### The Problems of Vocabulary

The problems of technical terminology in such a theological study are difficult. Almost every term that can be used in analysis or generalization has suffered at one time or another from being a party word freighted with the emotions of controversy. "Liberal," "conservative," "modern," "orthodox," "scientific," or "scholastic" all connote far more than they denote. Yet their use is unavoidable. One word that most badly needs refurbishing is "liberal." Liberalism is generally accepted today as the description of a particular type of Protestant theology which emerged at the end of the nineteenth century, and, as such, has come in for all the brickbats the twentieth century has poured upon the nineteenth. Yet its meaning is far broader and is a necessary characterization of one of the most basic features of all modern theologies. "Liberal" means just what its Latin root implies—"freedom." Liberalization was the progressive freeing of the religious life from domination by set formulas whose truth was validated by the claim of authority from Scripture or church, instead of a free investigation in the light of human knowledge and experience. Freedom to examine and evaluate the Christological formulas instead of just accepting them is a basic and continuing feature of modern theology. To speak of "liberalism" or a process of "liberalization" is not to imply that the whole history of modern theology was working to produce the liberalism of Ritschl and Harnack. Liberalization is, rather, one of the basic responses of Christian thought to the rise of secularism.

Similarly, a word must be spoken about "secularism" itself. "Secularization" is used here to describe the progressive release of human existence and thought from overt religious control. This movement is too all-embracing to allow for a simple verdict. Its relation to Biblical faith can be established, yet the problems that secularization has posed for the intellectual and institutional life of Christianity are immense. Secularization has forced theology in the modern world more often to think apologetically than simply descriptively. The final verdict on the meaning of secularism for Christian faith remains to be written by history. Our words are inevitably penultimate. Yet some things are now clear. Whereas the Reformation was a movement within Christendom to realign its piety and theology in the light of its revelatory sources, modern theology has been the attempt to reorient the faith in the light of an emerging world of man and his powers. The concern around which theology is to be shaped is no longer Scripture versus tradition but Gospel versus world.

The evaluation of the importance of the philosophies and theologies that are found in modernity in relation to the unfolding of Christology is rendered difficult because the process we are viewing is far from complete. For the student of Christology in the early church there are certain bench marks by which the stages of historical development can be established. No matter what a historian may believe about the final truth of the great creedal decisions of Nicaea and Chalcedon, they do mark set points in reference to which developments can be measured. The contribution of a particular writer may be analyzed in relation to the doctrinal settlements that emerged. Yet to the historian of modernity, particularly the historian of Protestant theology, no such bench marks are available. Modern theology has not drawn toward any consensus, nor is it likely to do so. Change and multiplicity are the order of the day. They have been since the advent of modern theology, and nothing gives us reason to believe this will change. For this reason the use of the term "orthodox" is possible only if it is given careful definition. In modern terms, "orthodoxy" can best be used as a descriptive rather than an evaluate idea. To speak of the Christological orthodoxy of classical Protestantism at the beginning of the modern period is to describe a set of doctrinal affirmations that had become normative for the church in the sixteenth and seventeenth centuries. These great affirmations about the person and work of Christ stemmed historically from the ecumenical councils of the early church and the work of certain medieval theologians. They had been taken into Protestantism by the Reformers and were now being refined and reoriented in the light of the Protestant doctrine of the authority of Scripture. This system of doctrine constitutes the Christology of the great Lutheran and Reformed theologians of the immediate post-Reformation era. This is the orthodoxy in the light of which the new Christologies of the early modern period were formed. Orthodoxy is not used here in its traditional evaluative sense of implying right belief, or belief in conformity with revelation. Actually, one of the first questions raised by the new Christologies was whether the orthodoxy of classical Protestantism was in conformity with the revelatory events witnessed to by Scripture. They were actually questioning the orthodoxy of "orthodoxy." But to put the matter in just this way would be to create confusion. So the term "orthodoxy" is to be left as a descriptive term characterizing the doctrinal systems of the church at the time when the modern reformulation was undertaken.

## Christological Orthodoxy

By the beginning of modern times, the church had evolved a complex picture of Jesus Christ. This picture reflected not only the revelatory events themselves but also the long history of interaction between Christianity and culture. The Christological orthodoxy that emerged was an intellectually sophisticated structure. Centuries of theological reflection had developed an amazing subtlety of thought on many points of doctrine. The slow, careful reflection of the church on the meaning of its confession of Jesus Christ as Lord had produced a Christology that gave every indication of being a stable and enduring part of Christian faith. Three major doctrinal affirmations were the basis for understanding the person and work of Christ in the Protestant orthodox teachers of the sixteenth and seventeenth centuries: the doctrine of the Trinity, the doctrine of the divine and human natures of Christ, and the doctrine of the substitutionary atonement. The notion that any of these doctrines were "interpretation" or "theory" about divine revelation was largely unknown save to a few critical minds. These doctrines were "revealed doctrines," sharing fully in the authority of Scripture and of divine revelation itself. What the Reformed dogmatician Bullinger said of the doctrine of the Trinity could well be said of the other doctrines also: "Since the unity in trinity of the Deity is simply and plainly taught in Holy Scripture, it is fair that we should agree with Scripture and not investigate inquisitively or seek full knowledge in this life, of that which God has revealed."[1] All that modern historical study has made so commonplace concerning the tension between Biblical theology and that of the fathers and the ecumenical creeds had been scarcely more than intimated by the seventeenth century. With the advantage of hindsight, it is possible to look to the critical theology of the Ockhamist tradition, or the historical scholarship of the Renaissance humanists, or the Biblical theology of the Reformers to see a challenge being raised to the hegemony of the traditional Christology doctrines. But until the advent of modern times there was no broad or sustained challenge to orthodoxy in matters of Christology. There were powerful spiritual and intellectual forces keeping any critical movement in check. The tradition of Christological conservatism continued strong in Protestantism. As late as the nineteenth century, which witnessed the most startling advances in the reformulation of Christology, religion on the popular level and in its main institutional forms remained firmly attached to the doctrines of Christological orthodoxy.

The force and the tenacity of conservatism in Christology reflect not only the formal doctrinal pronouncements of the churches, both Catholic and Protestant, but also the deep involvement of these doctrines in the piety of Christianity. Simply to speak of the doctrine of the Trinity, the divine and human natures of Christ, or the atonement as concerns only in books of school theology is to miss the real force they possessed. They had become basic to the liturgy, hymnody, and personal piety of Christians. Whether it be the fourth-century hymns of Ambrose and Prudentius, or a hymn such as Reginald Heber's "Holy, Holy, Holy!" God was praised in three Persons as blessed Trinity. The atonement had been sung by Bernard of Clairvaux in "O Sacred Head, Now Wounded," and in Augustus Toplady's "Rock of Ages, Cleft for Me." The liturgy and hymnody of Advent and Christmas abound in references to the divine and human natures of Christ. The fierceness with which these doctrines were defended witnesses to the living force they had in Christian life. The modern tendency to see theological doctrines as somehow aloof from, or even antithetical to, piety blinds us to the intimate way in which piety and doctrine were interwoven. Reinterpretation of the Christological center of Christian piety required not only a new intellectual schema but a new form of religious consciousness. Only as men were able to view the revelatory event of Jesus Christ separately from their basic doctrinal formulations could a new theology be born. The intellectual analysis reflects and is shaped by the more basic changes that have come with the growth of new forms of human consciousness.

Modern historical scholarship has displayed a richness and inclusiveness in the Christology of the fathers, the Reformers, and their orthodox interpreters of the sixteenth and seventeenth centuries. The great issues of theology were pursued with a passion and a profundity that make our modern efforts seem but a pale shadow of the real. Although there was much in the theology of Protestant orthodoxy that could well be counted arbitrary and sterile, there developed what has been rightly called "a truly practical theology." It was a theology related to the life of the church as it sought to bring itself into obedience to the Word. The early modernizers of doctrine were unaware of this richness but apprehended only the arbitrary and the narrow. One need only start with Servetus' *On the Errors of the Trinity,* for example, to see that what is rejected is really a caricature of patristic doctrine. The more appreciative judgment of historic theologies that modern scholarship has given us was not a possibility for them. Often they did not have adequate texts or scholarly tools. Historical theology as it is known today was only getting under way in the later eighteenth century.

But more important, the early modernizers of theology were caught in a spiritual struggle against the tyranny of a theology they found intellectually and morally distorting. It was a struggle against a theology enforced by the power of state and church. In such a struggle the richer more inclusive perspective of those who live on the other side of the struggle was not seen. To look at the doctrines at the center of concern for the early liberals is not the same as viewing orthodox theology.

Three basic theological questions were at stake in Christological orthodoxy: (1) How is Jesus Christ related to God the Father? (2) How is he related to us men? (3) How is he the Savior of men? The first two questions were the focus of theological concern in the patristic age. They led to the formulation of the doctrine of the Trinity, which sets forth the relation of the Father to the Son, and the doctrine of the divine and human natures of Christ, which established the relation of the Christ to mankind. These doctrines were given full dogmatic status in the ecumenical councils of the church at Nicaea in 325, Constantinople in 381, and Chalcedon in 451; and there were repeated clarifications at other times as heresies arose. The answer to the third question was of great interest to the early church also. A number of atonement doctrines are to be found in the patristic literature, but none of these doctrines ever reached full dogmatic authority in antiquity. The answer to this question which was basic for Western Christendom by the beginning of modern times was the doctrine of substitutionary atonement developed by the great medieval theologian Anselm of Canterbury. Even though the Anselmian teaching did not reach full dogmatic authority in any church council, it provided the basis from which Protestant orthodox theology developed its doctrine of atonement.

Historically the doctrines of the Trinity and the two natures of Christ developed out of the church's attempt to explicate and defend its basic confession of Jesus Christ as Lord. This confession is twofold. In Jesus Christ, God the Lord is truly present at work for the salvation of man, and this One in whom God is present is also a true man, Jesus of Nazareth. During the second century the Apologists attempted to express and defend this confession with a Logos Christology. Jesus Christ is a man who is the incarnate Logos. The Apologists conceived of the Logos as subordinate to God the Father. The Logos and the Spirit are emanations or expressions of God, and as such, subordinate. For a time during the second and third centuries this implicit subordinationism was not viewed as dangerous. It was only with the rise of the Arian heresy and its clear and polemic assertion of the inferiority of the Son to the Father that orthodoxy was defined in terms of the Son's being of one substance (homoousios) with the Father. To confess Christ as homoousios with the Father means he is not simply like God but is the very being of the Father. This formulation was the work of Athanasius whose party triumphed at the Council of Nicaea, although it took many years of struggle before the terms of the settlement were fully accepted. The issue that impelled Athanasius to insist on the homoousios formula was his doctrine of salvation. He argued that if God is not fully and personally present in Jesus Christ, then Christ cannot be the Savior. No subordinate, semi-divine being has the power of salvation. It is only as the Son is consubstantial, coequal and coeternal with that Father that he can be the Savior. The logic of Athanasius' position was eventually broadened to include the Holy Spirit and affirmed at Constantinople in 381.

If the church wanted to assert the full divinity of Christ, particularly in its Nicaean formulation, and yet maintain a rigorous monotheism, the doctrine of God which it had inherited from Judaism had to undergo major change. This process of change had been under way since the earliest beginnings of Christianity. The evolution of Christology and of the doctrine of God in the early church were inseparable. When the relation of the Son and the Spirit to the Father is defined, not as subordination, but as full equality, the unity of God is placed in an entirely new light. It was no longer possible as with the Apologists to speak of the one God, the Father, who revealed himself through the Son and the Spirit who were subordinate modes of his being. In the Trinitarian formulas of the fourth century, the one God was confessed in three coequal, coeternal Persons. Such a definition made the whole question of the divine unity much more complex. It is not enough to define the unity of God as simple, undifferentiated, arithmetic oneness. To do this would be to fall back into some form of monarchianism that ignored the separateness of Father, Son, and Spirit. The unity of God must be defined in such a way as to allow a differentiation of the Father from the Son, and the Son from the Spirit. Yet at the same time it had to be maintained that Father, Son, and Spirit are God. This problem was met in two ways by the patristic theologians. They maintained that the Father eternally begets the Son, and from the Father and Son together proceeds the Spirit. The unity of God is that of a mutually begetting triad whose very existence is dependent on its innerrelatedness. The Cappadocian fathers also introduced the doctrine of "perichoresis" or interpenetration of the divine Persons in the Trinity. Unlike finite persons the members of the Trinity are not delimited from one another by boundary lines. Rather, their being interpenetrates one another. In this way God can be thought of as one. According to Gregory of Nazianzus, God can be said to exist "undivided in divided Persons" (*Or.* 31, 14).

In its finished form the Trinitarian doctrine went beyond the Biblical materials in both form and content. It was deeply indebted, as indeed was the Christological dogma, to the philosophical and religious thought of Greco-Roman antiquity. But the church accepted and defended it as a proper and necessary interpretation of what the Bible teaches. The Trinitarian doctrine became the intellectual framework within which the church stated and defended its belief in the divinity of Christ. The Trinitarian conceptions of God and the divinity of Christ were so intimately related that to speak of one inevitably led to consideration of the other. To deny either of these doctrines was to deny the faith. To defend the doctrine of the Trinity was not to defend a particular speculative teaching about God. In the mind of the orthodox teachers, to defend the Trinity was to defend the very saving truth of Christian faith.

Once the divinity of Christ had been determined by the use of the term "homoousios" at Nicaea, the question of his humanity became the subject of new controversies. It had been clear since the anti-Gnostic struggles of the second century that

the church was firmly committed to belief in the full humanity
of Christ. This could not be compromised. But if Christ is the
incarnate second Person of the Trinity sharing fully in the divine attributes of omnipotence, omniscience, and omnipresence,
how can he also be man? Two alternatives were open, either
of which followed to its extreme led into heresy. One possibility
was to limit the humanity, or merge it with the divine nature.
In this way the unity of Christ's person was ensured, but at the
cost of making his human nature no longer fully like that of
other men. The second possibility was to maintain in the strict-
est way possible the integrity of both the divine nature and
the human nature in Christ. Yet such a thoroughgoing differentiation of the two natures made it impossible to account adequately for the unity of his person. At Chalcedon a formula
was set forth that sought to secure the values of both horns of
the dilemma. The use of the term "homoousios" was broadened.
Jesus Christ is homoousios not only with the Father but also
with the men he came to save.

> We confess one and the same our Lord Jesus Christ, and
> we all teach harmoniously [that he is] the same perfect in
> Godhead, the same perfect in manhood, truly God and truly
> man, the same of a reasonable soul and body; consubstantial
> . . . with us in manhood, . . . acknowledged in two natures
> without confusion, without change, without division, without
> separation—the difference of the natures being by no means
> taken away because of the union, but rather the distinctive
> character of each nature being preserved, and [each] combin-
> ing in one Person and *hypostasis*—not divided or separated
> into two Persons, but one and the same Son and only-begotten
> God, Word, Lord Jesus Christ.

The formula of Chalcedon was much clearer on what it rejected than on what it affirmed about the person of Christ. But
historically it had one overarching effect. It provided the context within which the person of Christ was to be understood.
The formula "two natures in one person" provided the framework for theological reflection and for Christian worship. The
formula pointed to the mystery of incarnation by excluding
every attempt to compromise either Christ's divine or human
nature.

During the patristic age the church reached no consensus on the doctrine of salvation. A variety of teachings were current to explain how Christ is Savior. There was the so-called "deification" doctrine which had been so important for Athanasius. By the very act of incarnation human nature had been linked with the divine nature and from it received the gift of immortality. Another teaching of great prominence among the fathers pictured Christ as redeeming mankind by giving himself as a ransom to trick the devil and, having come into his power, then destroying him. The recapitulation theory was also current which saw in Christ the representative Man who overcame the powers of sin and death men face at each stage of life from beginning to end. There was also a substitutionary atonement doctrine which focused attention on the cross as the sacrificial death of Christ in which he bore the penalty of human sin. These various interpretations of salvation were not systematically delineated. They were often found together in one writer despite divergences and even contradictions between them. It was only in the Middle Ages that systematic clarification was undertaken. During this time there had been a gradual elimination of many of the doctrines of salvation found in the fathers, until in Anselm's *Cur Deus Homo?* (ca. 1097) the doctrine of substitutionary atonement was given central importance. There is considerable New Testament evidence for conceiving of the death of Christ as a sacrifice made on behalf of mankind to atone for the sins of man. However, the exact form that Anselm gave to the doctrine went beyond the Biblical materials, drawing on ideas from the medieval penitential system and legal codes. Human sin, Anselm argued, is an affront to the majesty and honor of God. Man, however, cannot render satisfaction to God, for the most a man can do is fulfill his duty of perfect obedience to God. The satisfaction that man must make is infinite; the satisfaction that man can make is null. Man can only be restored by a God-man. In his sinless life the God-man is simply fulfilling his duty toward God. Satisfaction for the sins of mankind comes from his free offering of his life to God on the cross. This free surrender of the life of the God-man has infinite merit which can be applied to men to free them from the sentence of death.

This doctrine was not without its critics in the Middle Ages. Abelard, Anselm's contemporary, posed a very different version of Christ's role as Savior. Both Luther and Calvin admitted the substitutionary doctrine of the atonement to Protestant theology, although it was not the sole conception of soteriology, nor the most basic.[2] Calvin warned against a too-deep probing into the whys and wherefores of God's activity, which Anselm had undertaken with such great certainty. Calvin admonishes, "After hearing that Christ was divinely appointed to bring relief to miserable sinners, whoso overleaps these limits gives too much indulgence to a foolish curiosity."[3] Nevertheless, by the seventeenth century Protestant theologians were talking of the absolute necessity of vicarious sacrifice as the only ground for salvation. The Reformed teacher Amandus Polanus expressed the mind of his orthodox contemporaries (1624) when he spoke of the mediatorial office of Christ:

> The Mediator of reconciliation between God and fallen men is the *persona* who intervenes midway between a God angry at their sins and men the sinners, in order that by his own merit and satisfaction he may obtain from God for men and effectively bestow on them grace, remission of sins and all things necessary for salvation and also eternal salvation itself.[4]

The Christology of the ecumenical creeds and the atonement doctrine of Anselm came into Protestantism from late medieval Catholicism. The reception of these doctrines by the Reformers and the theologians of Protestant orthodoxy did effect certain changes as they sought their Biblical basis. Yet it was in Christology that there existed the deepest and most significant continuity between the Reformation and Catholicism. The principal reinterpretations were in the doctrine of the work of Christ. In their polemics against the Mass as the continuation and completion of Christ's work, the Reformers sought a Biblical schema within which to interpret the work of Christ. This was first developed by Luther and Calvin in the doctrine of the threefold office of Christ as Prophet, Priest, and King. This schema brought the full picture of the life, death, resurrection, and coming again of Christ into an inclusive doctrine based on Scripture. Its main thrust was to show the completeness of God's provision for human salvation. Salvation was complete in Christ, and neither man nor church can add anything to it. Although the schema of Prophet, Priest, and King was a broadly inclusive one, allowing place for the role of Jesus as teacher as well as atoning sacrifice, the full potential of this interpretation was never realized by the theologians of orthodoxy. Because of its focus on justification as the grounds of salvation, Protestantism tended increasingly to narrow its view of Christ's work to that of his death and resurrection as the grounds of his saving power. As the Second Helvetic Confession (1561) puts it, "Therefore, solely on account of Christ's sufferings and resurrection God is propitious with respect to our sins" (Ch. XV). The life of Jesus is not viewed as a moral example for the believer as much as a part of his work of vicarious satisfaction. Christ's actual obedience to the law during his lifetime is an integral part of the righteousness he imparts to the believer. As Johannes Wollebius (1586–1629) said, "But his actual obedience is not only a necessary condition of Christ as priest, but also a part of his satisfaction and merit."[5] The Anselmian doctrine itself underwent modification by the Protestant orthodox teachers. They rejected Anselm's use of the medieval penitential and legal codes as the basis for understanding sin and reconciliation. They insisted on Biblical metaphors derived from the legal codes of the Old Testament. However, these changes in organization and language in understanding the work of Christ did not change the basic features of the vicarious atonement thinking. The Lutheran David Hollaz (1646–1713) sees the active center of Christ's work in his cross.

> By the passive obedience [i.e., death on the cross] Christ transferred to Himself the sins of the whole world, and besides this suffered the punishments due them, by shedding His most precious blood, and meeting for all sinners the most ignominious death, in order that, to believers in Christ the Redeemer, sins might not be imputed for eternal punishment.[6]

The reception by Protestantism of these basic doctrines from Roman Catholicism did pose a problem. Catholicism was willing to build its theology on the basis of Scripture and tradition, but Protestantism had committed itself to the basis of Scripture alone. Could these doctrines be established fully on Biblical grounds? Orthodox Protestantism affirmed this possibility without exception. Certainly, the penal substitution theory of atonement could be related to the many Biblical references in both the Old and the New Testament. As later New Testament scholarship was to show, the Biblical teaching on atonement cannot be reduced simply to a theory of penal substitution. Yet such doctrine could be related to much New Testament and, in particular, Pauline theology. The problem of the doctrine of the Trinity and of the two natures of Christ was more difficult. Both these doctrines were committed to the use of non-Biblical terminology. In Roman Catholicism their validation was not in their unambiguous grounding in Scripture, although no one contested their Scriptural character, but in their validation by ecumenical councils and pope. The importance of church authority in supporting these doctrines had been increasingly emphasized in the late Middle Ages by the Ockhamist theology. The theology of the Reformation was confronted with the necessity of vindicating these doctrines as Scriptural. Both Luther and Calvin had no difficulty in finding Scriptural basis for these doctrines. Certainly they were not unaware that the exact terminology of these doctrines was not found in the Bible. Wollebius recognized this fact but did not believe it to be, therefore, an argument against the doctrine. "The words *persona,* triad, and *homoousious,* although not found in so many syllables in the Scriptures, are yet in agreement with the Scriptures and are usefully employed in the Church."[7] Calvin recognized that much of the speculative theologizing that had gone on about the Trinity could not be related to Scripture and, hence, cautioned restraint so that thinking would not go beyond the bounds of evidence. "Here if ever among the hidden mysteries of Scripture I recommend sober philosophizing of extreme restraint, with the further condition of great caution, lest either thought or tongue go beyond the point to which the territories of God's word extend."[8] Similarly, Luther in his repudiation of speculative philosophizing rejected probing too deeply into what is a mystery. The restraint in philosophizing about the Trinity and the natures of Christ by the Reformers themselves tended to be forgotten by later theologians. Philipp Melanchthon (1497–1560) attempted a speculative doctrine of the Trinity as did the Reformed teacher Bartholomew Keckermann. Their doctrine reinstituted the tradition of Trinitarian speculation started by Augustine. In his *Systematic Theology,* which appeared in 1602, Keckermann followed the Augustinian analogy to the Trinity found in the process of knowing. At no point did the theologians of Lutheran and Reformed orthodoxy believe that a doctrine of the Trinity could be reached by human reason. But reason can explicate the doctrine and vindicate its truth against the assaults of the anti-Trinitarians. Similarly, the doctrine of the two natures is inaccessible to reason, and "it should be divinely taught and proved from Scripture and received with the eyes of faith" (*Leiden Synopsis,* XXV, 2). However, analogical thinking can be of value in explication of the incarnation. Jerome Zanchius, a Reformed teacher (about 1585), believed it appropriate to reintroduce Augustine's speculations which liken the human nature of Christ to a garment; others experimented with the analogy of the fire in a glowing iron or of the relation of body and soul in a man. The speculative delineation of the union of the natures in Christ became the subject of a long and acrimonious debate between the Lutheran and the Reformed theologians. The arguments that animated the polemics of Protestant orthodoxy were by no means arguments about Biblical theology or exegesis in the historical sense. Although both sides to the arguments declared they were defending Biblical truth, their tools for analysis and their criteria for construction were derived from the school theology of the late Middle Ages. The caution of Calvin about a misleading natural theology based on analogy and the polemics of Luther against speculations and scholasticism were quickly forgotten by many of their followers in building the complex and rigid systems of Christology that characterized Protestantism in the sixteenth and seventeenth centuries.

## New Presbyter and Old Priest

By the seventeenth century John Milton delivered the verdict of the new religious and political movements of his day on the spiritual tyranny of the official defenders of Reformed orthodoxy in his poem "On the New Forcers of Conscience Under the Long Parliament." Of the Scots divines who presided over this theology he said, "New Presbyter is but Old Priest writ Large." The orthodoxy of the Reformation threatened "to force our consciences that Christ set free," and to enforce itself with "plots and packings worse than those of Trent." Milton could well be joined in his protest against the hegemony of Protestant orthodoxy by all those committed to a liberalization of Christian doctrine from Servetus to Kant. For them, Protestantism was not an ally but an opponent which, at worst, resorted to banishment or the stake and, at best, to censorship and harassment. The modernizing movements in theology saw in classical Protestantism a foe no less dogmatic and arbitrary than Rome. The doctrines of the Trinity, of the two natures of Christ, and of the substitutionary atonement against which these early modernizers of Christology revolted were clearly and firmly established at the heart of a Protestant orthodoxy that was not inclined to grant freedom of judgment that could imperil these central truths of the faith.

Over against this reaction to the theological heritage of classical Protestantism stands another fact with which any estimate of the role of the Reformation in modern theology must be concerned. It was only within Protestantism that the new theology was able to arise. Despite opposition and, later, only a grudging acceptance, it was on Protestant grounds that the dialogue with modernity could be creative. The response of Roman Catholicism to the rise of modernity during the sixteenth through the eighteenth century was rejection. Catholicism found no substantial grounds for dialogue or accommodation in the modern religious consciousness until our own times. However, Protestantism in a way that exceeded either the intention or the scope of the Reformers themselves created a potential for change by undercutting the institutional and theological unity that had pervaded Western Christendom in the Middle Ages. The direct heirs of the Reformation in the major churches of classical Protestantism did not recognize or accept this potential for creative interaction with the new intellectual and social forces being let loose in their time. This potential was first recognized by those who stood on the fringes of official Protestantism, or, at times, only by its critics.

Popular estimates of the Reformation tend to overlook the complexity of its attitudes on freedom of thought and faith. Freedom of thought, separation of church and state, and the right of individual interpretation of Scripture are often pictured as stemming directly from the Reformation. The focal point of the new religious movement of the sixteenth century, it is argued, was in awakening the Protestant principle of prophetic criticism against dogmatic theologies and sacrosanct institutions. This principle was at work in all the great movements of social, political, and intellectual liberation that have characterized the modern world. Such a view of the Reformation contains a truth mixed with an error. There is a legitimate sense in which the Reformation with its rediscovery of the Bible and the doctrine of justification by faith was a vital factor in the unfolding of the modern world. But this contribution was only made slowly and indirectly as the Reformation heritage was brought into relation with other historical forces let loose by the Renaissance and the rise of modern science. Initially it is clear that the freedom for which the Reformers contended was freedom from "popish error," not the highly individualistic freedom of the eighteenth-century political theorists. The notion that the Reformation championed total freedom of opinion and was the basis of modern liberalism in religion and politics comes, in part, from Roman Catholic polemics against the Reformation. In the Restoration theology of Catholicism, following the French Revolution, it became the style to trace the troubles of the modern world back to the chaos caused by the principles of 1789, which in turn rest upon the Reformers.[9] In a somewhat more sophisticated fashion, Jacques Maritain pictures Luther as a key figure whose thought "dominates the modern world, and governs all the problems which torment it."[10] It is Luther who stands behind the perverted intellectualism and voluntarism of the modern world and who can be related, by Maritain at least, to "the Kantian shrivelled up in his autonomy, . . . the Nietzschean giving himself curvature of the spine in his effort to jump beyond good and evil, the Freudian cultivating his complexes, . . . a disciple of M. Gide viewing himself with gloomy enthusiasm in the mirror of his freedom."[11] Maritain had to admit in a remarkably telling footnote that his view of Luther's importance was derived, "not theoretically and according to Luther, but actually and according to truth."[12]

By contrast, German romanticism found in the Reformation the sources of creativity in the modern world. Fichte saw Luther as "the prototype of modern times." Lessing invoked the spirit of Luther, the man who rebelled against church and emperor in the name of truth personally apprehended, against the orthodox literalism which claimed to be the true heir of Luther.

> The true Lutheran does not wish to be defended by Luther's writings but by Luther's spirit; and Luther's spirit absolutely requires that no man may be prevented from advancing in the knowledge of the truth according to his own judgment.[13]

Whether one finds with the Roman Catholic polemics the torments or with romanticism the triumphs of modern man in the Reformation, one thing remains clear. Liberalism, whether it be perverse or creative, is an implication to be derived from the Reformers or a spirit elicited from their work. In both cases, these people are talking about what the Reformation became. Or perhaps, more accurately, in the case of Lessing, he was stating what the Reformation should become to the German people. For at the time he wrote this, Lessing was engaged in a fight against the literalistic orthodoxy of Chief Pastor Goeze of Hamburg, who could lay claim to standing in direct succession to the Reformation theology. As a critic standing outside the Lutheran establishment, Lessing was forced to appeal to the "spirit of Luther" rather than to "Luther's writings." This distinction is an important key to the difference between implications that arise from the Reformation and the concrete reception of the Reformation traditions in the sixteenth through the eighteenth century. The theologians of Lutheran and Reformed orthodoxy stood in the minds of their contemporaries as the heirs of the Reformers. When the framers of the Book of Concord argued from what "Dr. Luther maintained," they believed they spoke in the light of Luther's word and spirit both. Similarly Wollebius, Voetius, Turretin, and the other great Reformed theologians looked to Calvin as the first and greatest in the theological tradition of which they were a part. The theologians of classical Protestant orthodoxy did not believe that the Reformation abolished dogmatic theology but simply put it on its proper foundation from which it had strayed.

Modern historical scholarship has put the innovative and conservative aspects of the Reformation into perspective. The Christology of the Reformation exists in a tension between traditional dogma and the new critical principle. Albrecht Ritschl, Karl Holl, and others have explored this tension in Luther's writings, while more recently Wilhelm Niesel, Edward Dowey, and others have described it in Calvin's theology. Ritschl distinguishes in Luther's Christology the theoretical and religious estimates of Christ.[14] Theoretically—i.e., in formal theological interpretation—Luther seeks to establish the old Christology through the doctrine of the sharing of the attributes of the two natures. This side of Luther's Christology became the basis for the distinctive doctrine of the Lutheran orthodox teachers. Luther's religious estimate of Christ does not depend upon this rigorous and exclusive interpretation of the doctrine of the two natures. Religiously the estimation of Christ as God implies personal trust in him. Merely intellectual assent to propositions about the divinity of Christ is not a sufficient basis for Christian faith. The treatment of the second article of the Creed in Luther's Small Catechism shows this tension between the traditional description of divinity and its personal apprehension. "I believe that Jesus Christ, true God, begotten of the Father from eternity, and also true man, born of the virgin Mary, is my Lord, who has redeemed me, . . . delivered me and freed me from all sins." The traditional predicates of divinity are retained, yet the emphasis is broadened to include their actual relation to the believer. The attributes of Christ are considered from the perspective of what they mean "for me."

By his emphasis on personal apprehension of Christ, Luther opened the way to a modern reconstruction of Christology which proceeds from religious experience and is described in practical terms. Although Luther retains the traditional formulas, his religious vision of Christ is not dependent on them.[15] The tension between the religious and the theoretical estimates of Christ was dissolved by the theologians of Lutheran orthodoxy. They gave dominance to Luther's theoretical estimate of Christ. They failed to explore the implications of Luther's thought which pointed far beyond the reaffirmation of the traditional Christology to provide the grounds for a modern interpretation. Even though the personalistic, religious view of Christ lived on in Lutheran piety and hymnody, it was subordinated in formal theologizing to the continuous refining of the doctrine of the two natures. Only in the light of the intellectual revolution of modernity was the personal, religious apprehension of Christ to play a constructive role in theological reflection.

Modern Calvin scholarship has revealed a tension between his doctrine of authority and revelation, on the one hand, and his use of traditional doctrines on the other. Calvin's theology is not simply the reconstruction of a late medieval dogmatics on the basis of the authority of Scripture alone. His thought is not to be understood as being connected through the logical elaboration of some single principle, such as the doctrine of predestination. Rather, as Niesel contends, Calvin is seeking to lead men in their understanding of Scripture so they may come to know Jesus Christ. Calvin's theology is Christocentric and derives its structure from the elaboration of Christ's meaning rather than through any traditional scholastic structure or creedal definition.[16] The authority of Scripture for Calvin is not that of a kind of dogmatic compend which theology simply makes explicit. Man's knowledge of God is existential. It is found when the words of the Bible are brought into living connection with the work of the Spirit to bear their witness to the living Word. This knowledge of God, as Dowey argues, is not simply intellectual information about God.[17] Knowledge of God is itself the gift of life touching man on every level of his being. Traditional formulas, such as those of Nicaea and Chalcedon, may be guides to exegesis, but their authority is clearly secondary to the joint witness of Spirit and Scripture. By his insistence on the reality of Christ's humanity Calvin was opening the way to a fresh estimate of the importance of the historical Jesus for faith. Such an awareness of the reality of Jesus' human life prepared the way for the modern historical study of the Gospels. Theology must let the Scriptures speak in terms of themselves. Calvin raises the sternest strictures against speculation in theology. The word of man, even if from wise and pious men, must be silent when in the power of the Spirit the Word of God is present.

Side by side with this aspect of Calvin stands the witness to the rigidity and dogmatism long associated with his name. He speaks of the authors of Scripture as being the instruments or organs of the Holy Spirit by which God dictated Scripture.[18] As doctrinal controversy hardened his thought, Calvin turned increasingly to this view of the Bible. His tragic intransigence in resisting the anti-Trinitarianism of Servetus reveals that he was far from willing to reconsider the Trinitarian formulas in the light of a new interpretation of Scripture. His rigid definitions of the doctrine of the two natures of Christ put him in opposition not only to the humanistic sectarians but to the Lutherans also. Reformed orthodoxy emphasized the verbal inspiration of Scripture, the doctrine of predestination, and the penal substitution doctrine of the atonement. These developments obscured the more dynamic thrust of Calvin's thought. The potential for developing a theology able to reform itself constantly in the light of the witness of Spirit and Scripture was lost in a scholastic methodology. Under the pressure of the times, the Reformed theologians built a closely integrated intellectual structure to state and defend their faith. In doing this they blunted Calvin's keenest insights into the doctrines of revelation and salvation. The Christological center was replaced by the doctrine of predestination. The dynamic interplay of Spirit and Scripture was replaced by legalistic literalism in interpreting the Bible.

This historical analysis is in its details still open to debate. This is not an attempt to settle the issues finally. Yet this analysis does place in perspective the tension between innovation and conservatism in the Reformers. On the innovative side Luther and Calvin loosed spiritual and intellectual forces whose scope far exceeded their own expectations or the capacities of their followers. By giving basic importance to the religious impact of Christ on the life of the believer rather than to the acceptance of intellectual formulas, Luther opened the way to the Christology of Semler, Schleiermacher, and Ritschl. Calvin, with his emphasis on the primacy of Scripture as the witness to revelation, opened the way to a critical evaluation of early Catholicism and the creeds in the light of primitive Christianity. The Calvinistic emphasis on the reality of Christ's humanity became an invaluable presupposition for the modern interest in the historical Jesus. Yet these were implications that did not become immediately evident in the sixteenth century or for some time afterward to the followers of the Reformation theology. The political as well as intellectual struggles between the forces of the Reformation and of Roman Catholicism in the sixteenth century and, in the next century, the Thirty Years' War provided no adequate atmosphere for investigating the innovative potential of Protestantism. Only as the new world view of modern science and the new view of man in modern philosophy with its growing consciousness of history opened a fresh approach to the doctrinal structure of orthodoxy was the potential of Protestantism for dialogue to be realized.

*Chapter II*

# PIONEERS

# OF A NEW WAY

*Asking the Right Questions*

The basis for gaining new knowledge is the ability to ask the right question. The beginnings of the modern view of Christ were made by men who posed the crucial questions about the Christological orthodoxy of their day. These men were the rationalistic, humanistic thinkers of the Reformation age: Michael Servetus (1511–1553), Sebastian Castellio (1515–1563), Bernardino Ochino (1487–1564), Lelius Socinus (1525–1562), and Faustus Socinus (1539–1604). They were pioneers of a new way. Like pioneers, they did not reach their promised land. Like prophets, they received no honor save that of exile, imprisonment, and death. What emerged from their work was not an enduring, nor could one even say a distinctively modern, Christology. Their theology did not achieve systematic completion, nor even a high measure of inner consistency. Rather, their contribution came from standing on the boundaries of Christian thought in their time and posing for the church crucial questions it had never thought to ask. The age of the Reformation was one in which the most basic questions were being raised about the nature of the gospel and the centers of religious authority. These rationalistic, humanistic thinkers of the left wing of the Reformation pressed their questioning beyond the boundaries to which Protestantism had come. They believed the

35

Protestant Reformation had been too timid in pursuit of its Biblical critique of churchly orthodoxy. They believed Protestantism had become so obsessed with its pursuit of *sola fide,* that it had failed to carry through on its examination of theology in the light of its other great principle—*sola Scriptura.* These humanistic thinkers raised the crucial questions about the doctrines of the Trinity, of the two natures of Christ, and of the substitutionary atonement. Are these really Scriptural doctrines? How do these doctrines stand before the judgment of man's reason? Is there any basis for holding that the creedal orthodoxy of the patristic age is an adequate, let alone final, interpretation of the meaning of Christ? These questions were revolutionary. Equally revolutionary was the way in which these thinkers rebuilt theology by a combination of Biblicism and rationalism. Doctrine had to be tested before the twin tribunals of Bible and human reason. Their hope was to regain a faith both rational and Biblical. Such a faith they believed could restore the purity and power of primitive Christianity.

Although left-wing theologians were critical of "standard brand" Protestantism, they did share common concerns. With Luther and Calvin they struggled against the authority of church and empire for freedom to hold and express their deepest religious conviction. Their Biblicism and their Christ-centered piety made common cause with Protestantism's rejection of all man-made devotions and doctrines. They wanted to read the Bible in terms of itself instead of through the churchly interpreters of the Middle Ages. Even the lives and personal destinies of many of the humanistic theologians crossed and recrossed those of the Reformers. Sebastian Castellio early had a friendship with Calvin, who gave him a job as a schoolteacher and may even have contemplated appointing him a preacher until doctrinal differences separated them. Early in life Michael Servetus served in Basel under John Oecolampadius until his anti-Trinitarianism became clear. Lelius Socinus had tried to engage Calvin in a scholarly dialogue over the resurrection of man, only to be rebuffed. Tragically it was in Protestant Geneva, under the leadership of Calvin, that Servetus was to pay with his life for his beliefs. Common starting points did not finally prevent deep and tragic differences.

The theology of the left wing is indebted not only to Reformation Biblicism but also to the critical theology of the late Middle Ages. The intellectual roots of both their anti-Trinitarian polemic and doctrine of God go deeply into nominalistic theology. The great synthesis between faith and reason reared in the high Middle Ages by Thomas Aquinas (1225–1274) had been under attack for some time. In the works of Duns Scotus (1264–1308) and William of Ockham (1300–1349) the Thomistic synthesis was criticized. The new critical theology emphasized the volitional rather than the rational character of the divine being. God, they argued, existed and acted in a particular manner simply because he so willed. Other modes of existence and action were equally possible. There is no rational necessity in the divine life. God is what he is not because it is reasonable but simply because he has chosen to be that way. On these grounds there is little possibility of apprehending the divine being by reason. Truth is known by the act of will in accepting the truth about God taught by the church. The great undergirding structure of a natural theology so characteristic of the system of Thomas was increasingly dissolved. In its place came the ever stronger appeal to submit to the authority of the church. Because of its divinely given authority, what the church teaches must be accepted as true even when its rational basis becomes increasingly unclear. This appeal to authority was not the only possible response to the critical investigation of the rationality of Christian doctrine. In the hands of those who rejected church authority it could become a powerful weapon for undermining doctrine. In the face of the irrationality of a doctrine like that of the Trinity, a person can either glory in his *sacrificium intellectus* in accepting it or he can reject it as irrational. Sebastian Castellio rejected Trinitarianism because of its sheer violation of the basic laws of "grammar, dialectics and arithmetic that three is three and one, one, and if it is three, it is not one, and if it is one, it is not three."[1] To violate such a rule in thinking about God is nothing commendable, nor is it to be called some superior form of faith. It is only to become no "better informed than an animal."

The most decisive force on the theologians of the left-wing Reformation came from the Renaissance. The Renaissance was a complex movement in the history of Western man. Any catch-word, even the term "Renaissance" itself, is bound to obscure the rich and varied patterns of thought that came from the rein-troduction into Western Christendom of humanistic traditions from Greco-Roman antiquity. The turning point for religious thought came with the introduction of the Christian humanism of Desiderius Erasmus (1466–1536) and the more moderate voices of the northern Renaissance into the arena of theological reflection. In the early centuries of Christendom the church fathers had turned from the humanistic side of classical antiquity, while drawing heavily from its religious and speculative phi-losophy.

The "rebirth" of the Renaissance was not simply that of clas-sical learning but of humanism, a faith in the freedom and po-tential goodness of man. It was the rediscovery of a vision of man that had come from the sages of Greece and Rome, a vision long forgotten amid the pessimism of late medieval piety which was to light the way to a new vision of Christ. The hu-manism of the Renaissance provided the perspective from which a trenchant criticism of medieval piety with its religion of in-dulgences, pilgrimages, fastings, prescribed prayers, holy days, and holy relics was made. Erasmus counseled men to turn from this religion of illusion to the religion of reality. "You honor a likeness of Christ's face that has been crudely sketched out of rock or wood, or else daubed in paint; much more to be honored is that likeness of his mind which has been portrayed in the words of the Gospels."[2] In its basis the humanistic criti-cism reached far beyond the abuses of medievalism to the doc-trine of original sin.

The interpretation of the Fall of man given by Augustine as a result of his controversy with Pelagius had become a funda-mental part of the Christian view of man. In the theology of the Reformation the Augustinian interpretation of original sin was given fresh prominence. Luther, Calvin, and the theologians of post-Reformation orthodoxy worked carefully to rid the doc-trine of original sin of any compromises with its severity that may have crept in during the past. Original sin does not mean simply that men break the law of God; it also implies a bondage of the will and a darkness of the mind that keep men from either knowing or following the will of God. As Martin Chemnitz (1522–1586), the great dogmatician of Lutheran orthodoxy, put it: "Original sin is the lack of original righteousness, that is, there is in men born of the seed of man a loss of light in the mind, a turning away of the will from God, a stubbornness of the heart, so that they cannot obey the Law of God, following the fall of Adam."[3] The doctrine of original sin did not deny freedom to men in their everyday life, or the ability to fulfill, in outward action at least, the civil law. But before the all-important question of human salvation, man is impotent. He is unable to know or choose the truth of God save as aided by the power of the Holy Spirit. The reflection of philosophers, poets, historians, and lawyers about human vices falls short of what Scripture teaches about sin. "Reason recognizes only those sins which consist either in the external actions or in the excess of wicked desires, that is, it understands the fruits of sin to some extent. But Scripture shows the root itself, that is, it charges the entire natural man with sin which is called original sin."[4] The separation between the Renaissance humanists and the Protestant Reformers had been signaled by the polemic exchange between Luther and Erasmus over the freedom of the will. By the time Chemnitz wrote, the distinction between philosophical reflections on virtue and the Christian doctrine of sin had become absolute, so he could treat the role of philosophy with condescension. "Although philosophy is to be admired, yet it ignores the fact that even those who try to rule their instincts with some degree of diligence often have the most grievous lapses. Theology, however, sets forth and explains the cause of sin, namely, the depravity of nature and the tyranny of Satan working in the sons of disobedience."[5]

The Christian humanism of Erasmus stands on the other side of this great divide between the philosophical and the theological view of man. The Christian Renaissance thinkers asserted a continuity between the classical philosophical view of man and pure, Biblical Christianity. They saw what the ancient sages had to say about virtue and vice as in continuity with the Biblical teachings on sin. Man is to deal with his tendency to sin by right reason, prayer, and discipline to strengthen the will. In his *Enchiridion,* a manual of instruction for the Christian life, Erasmus tells of those things which can strengthen and guide the believer in his struggle against sin. "Prayer, of course, is the more potent, for it is communication with Deity, but knowledge is no less necessary. . . . Knowledge puts the intellect in touch with salutary ideas."[6] The shaping of the mind with the best in human wisdom is preparation for receiving the knowledge of God's will in Scripture. Erasmus recommends the study of the literature of classical antiquity as a preparation for the Christian life. The truth about man and the good life cannot be divided between the misleading work of human reason and the truth of revelation. Reason and revelation are in continuity. To suppose that man is impotent to resist vice is the avenue not to faith and virtue but to fatalistic immorality. No matter how severely the mind is agitated by the passions, men must know "that none of these agitations of the mind are so turbulent that they cannot be curbed by rational control or channeled in the direction of virtue."[7] "This, therefore, is the only way to virtue: first, that you know yourself; second, that you act, not according to the passions, but the dictates of reason."[8] Erasmus' exegesis of Scripture allowed for a translation of his philosophical formula for salvation into a Biblical one. "Reason" is to be translated by the Biblical term "spirit" or "inner man." The highest vision of the life of virtue is found in Jesus Christ as described in Scripture. The teachings of Christ provide the perfect means of educating men to the life of virtue and piety, a life that constitutes the highest human joy. The ideal of man of classical antiquity is revealed in its fullness in Christ. The vision of man given in Christ is not an ideal rendered irrelevant by the impotence of man. With a telling turn of phrase Erasmus sums up his deepest convictions: "Just as Christ will not be mocked, by the same token He will not mock us."[9] To the man who follows Christ, strength will be given to overcome in the battle of sin. Human striving is not the futile struggle of man against a corrupt nature he cannot overcome. The struggle of man for salvation is the opening to a grace that allows him to overcome what he could never overcome on his own. The warfare of the

Christian against sin is not a vain struggle in which he is condemned to failure. This would be a mockery of man. You can find "some method of living which might help you achieve a character acceptable to Christ."[10]

Such a view of man opened the way to a reconception of Christ as Savior. In Erasmus himself this reorientation was only intimated. It remained for the anti-Trinitarians and Socinians to carry out the polemics against churchly orthodoxy, for polemics was a task Erasmus eschewed. While not denying the doctrines of the Trinity and of the two natures, he did effect a reorientation in Christology. It was a shift away from the vision of Christ as supernatural Savior and atoning sacrifice to that of moral teacher and exemplar, bringing to man a converting picture of life in obedience to God. The converting force of Christian faith is not in arcane doctrines. Although Erasmus speaks of Christian faith as "the philosophy of Christ," it is a philosophy that can be known by the most humble. "The sun itself is not as common and accessible to all as is the teaching of Christ."[11]

The distinctively modern note of the Erasmian humanism was faith in the rationality and goodness of man. This faith was not shared by the Reformers, and official Protestantism stood in adamant opposition to the modernization of doctrine that stemmed from that tradition. The new Christologies can be correlated with the unfolding of this faith in man's moral and rational powers. The Christology of Erasmus was only a beginning. It could still be understood in the light of the late medieval *devotio moderna* of the Brethren of the Common Life with its ideal of the imitation of Christ. But the emphasis on Christ as the revealer of a new life for man through a faith grounded in human moral and spiritual capacities opened the way for a recasting of orthodoxy that spread beyond the vision of the time. The humanistic scholars' love for authentic texts of Scripture and the fathers and the growing knowledge of the original language provided the basis for the search for a historical picture of Christ. Patient philosophical study and the rational weighing of historical evidences are keys to truth in religion as in other avenues of life. Such convictions became the grain of mustard seed from which a tree was to spring.

## Christ and the Anti-Trinitarians

Since the patristic age the significance of the historical Jesus had been absorbed into the doctrines of Trinity, incarnation, and atonement. Fathers and theologians of the Middle Ages had taken the Pauline word about knowing Christ "no longer after the flesh" to justify their concern for dogmatic interpretation at the expense of history. The starting point for the anti-Trinitarians of the sixteenth century was a challenge to this outlook. Theology had approached the question of Jesus' historical existence from belief in him as second Person of the Trinity incarnate. What conception of Christ would emerge if the question of his earthly life were approached from the other end? What if theology were to start with the picture of Jesus the man as given in the New Testament? Such questions were raised in the mind of a brilliant young Spanish student of law at the University of Toulouse, Michael Servetus. His mind had been stirred by a fresh encounter with the New Testament in the company of a student group seeking to grasp its message afresh. They discovered the Bible not as a set of proof texts for the doctrine of the church but as a witness to the wisdom and knowledge of God given through Christ. The picture of Christ and his religion that emerged in Servetus' mind stood in revolutionary contrast to that which he had been taught. He found in the New Testament no talk of the Trinity, or the *communicatio idiomatum*. Why, he asked, had theology become involved in speculating on such things? Its basic starting point was wrong.

> In investigating the holy mysteries of the divine Triad, I have thought one ought to start from the man: for I see most men approaching this lofty speculation about the Word without having any fundamental understanding of Christ, and they attach little or no importance to the man, and give the true Christ quite over to oblivion. But I shall endeavor to recall to their memories who the Christ is.[12]

This new starting point did not result in anything like the recent research into the life of Jesus. Discerning levels of tradition and analyzing mythological elements in the New Testament were still in the future. Here was the first and crucial step of freeing the interpretation of Christ from doctrinal domination, to have it carried forward on historical grounds.

There were other sources for the false religion reared in the name of Christ. The church, argued Servetus, had not only been wrong in approaching the doctrine of Christ speculatively instead of historically; it had used the wrong sorts of intellectual tools. The church had forsaken the clear meaning of Scripture for the subtleties of Greek philosophy. "And this plague of philosophy was brought upon us by the Greeks, for they above all other men are most given to philosophy; and we, hanging upon their lips, have also become philosophers."[13] Instead of explicating the meaning of Scripture, this philosophizing had obscured it. For Servetus, Castellio, and the Socinians, the nub of the problem lies in the terminology used in the doctrines of the Trinity and of the two natures. When the term "person" is used it necessarily implies a distinct being. To speak of three Persons in the Trinity is unavoidably to speak of three gods, which is obvious nonsense. In Servetus' estimate, the believer who is "unwilling to misuse the word 'Persons' " must inevitably conclude that when theologians declare that "one person is born of another, and one is breathed out by the others," they are talking about three distinct beings. Even the theologians themselves admit this. Servetus cites John Major (1469–1550) in his *Sentences*—a basic theological textbook of the day—as admitting "a plurality of beings, a plurality of entities, a plurality of Essences, a plurality of *Ousias.*" Such thinking leads to a conclusion for Servetus far at odds with that of Major. For Servetus, when such language is used strictly it implies "a plurality of Gods."[14]

The left-wing theologians aimed to correct the errors that had come into theology. As the title of Servetus' major work indicated—*On the Errors of the Trinity*—they wanted to return belief in the divinity of Christ to its proper basis. In reading the New Testament and the pre-Nicene theologians, they discovered two basic ideas: the subordination of the Son to the Father and the lack of clear distinction between the "spirit of Christ" and the "Holy Spirit." They found no basis to support the doctrine of the Son and the Spirit being of one substance with the Father. In the light of their new reading of the New Testament they saw the orthodoxy defined at Nicaea not as the completion of earlier developments but as their distortion. They found no certain basis for a necessarily threefold separation of the various modes of divine activity. Faustus Socinus in his *Tract Concerning God, Christ, and the Holy Spirit* suggests, instead, a twofold separation between use of the word "God" in the absolute sense as applied to the Father himself, and "God" as used to characterize these beings who uniquely reveal God. They were willing to confess Christ as the Son of God, as the "form of God," and as the "express image of God." They accepted the virgin birth and believed the divine nature of Christ was revealed by his miracles and supremely by his resurrection. The difficulty remained in their positive statements on the divinity of Christ. They were clear in rejecting the traditional answer, yet it remained uncertain as to exactly what they would put in its place.

Servetus framed three propositions to summarize his view. First, the Christ is the man Jesus spoken of in Scripture. This seeming truism is in reality Servetus' statement of his new starting point. Christology must grow out of the historical witness of Scripture, not the speculations of the church. Second, this Christ is the Son of God because God is his Father, not a man. Servetus wanted to undercut all speculations about the eternal begetting of the Son by the Father. The Sonship of Christ is grounded in his conception, not in some imagined relationship within the life of God. Third, "Christ is God."[15] The possibility of making the statement "Christ is God" is based upon a distinction in the use of the term "God." Yet it was a distinction he had great difficulty clarifying. Despite his polemics against philosophical speculation, Servetus is forced to draw a philosophical distinction. The Christ, Servetus argues, is equal with God in power and is able to reveal fully the divine will, yet he is not identical with God in being. The Bible itself bears witness to a twofold application of the term "God." God is the term to characterize the one God. God is also applied to those beings through whom God reveals himself. This second sense of the term implies a derivative divinity. In other words, looked at from the human perspective, these beings are God. Ultimately they are not identical with the one, supreme God. The one God is himself unknown to men save through his revelation in Jesus Christ. Because of this it is natural for men to look upon Christ as God. It is through him we come to know God. Servetus sees his distinction in the uses of the term "God" as the explanation of the variations in the divine names used in the Old Testament. God the Father is called in the Old Testament *Yahweh*, whereas *El, Adonai,* and *Elohim* are names for those who carry out the work of God as Judge, King, or Lord. Christ is *Elohim*, not *Yahweh*.

> For Christ is Elohim our king who even from the beginning is *working salvation in the midst of the earth.* . . . He is the visible God who created the world, and appeared to Abraham, Isaac, and Jacob. He is the God of the law and the Prophets. . . . This very oracle of God was God himself. Yet it was the oracle, and not God himself, that came to be flesh.[16]

The manner in which the oracle of God became man Servetus explains through the doctrine of the divine self-emptying, or kenosis (Phil. 2:5–11). He breaks with the traditional interpretation of this doctrine. The divine self-limitation is not in the incarnation but in Christ's use of his divine powers. In his flesh Christ is a man, while in his spirit he is God. His existence "in the form of God" means "he had in himself an equal power of God." Yet he emptied himself and took upon himself the form of a servant by leading a life of humility instead of arrogating to himself the use of divine powers. The only times in which his divine existence was used were in the miracles. The exaltation of Christ in resurrection and ascension was his elevation to a place of equality with God in heaven, where he uses his divine powers fully.

Having gone this far in asserting the divinity of Christ, what keeps these men from using the Trinitarian confession? In fact, good questions can be raised as to whether the term "anti-Trinitarian" is itself entirely accurate. Was not their protest against distortions in theologizing about the Trinity made from the perspective of Biblical theology? In many respects Servetus, Castellio, and the others were simply carrying out a program of doctrinal reform that had at least been intimated by the leading Protestant Reformers at one time or another. Why, then, did such a deep cleft separate the left-wing theologians from the Protestants of their day? There are a number of *ad hominem* arguments that can be made. Servetus was a sharp-tongued person who upbraided his opponents as Pharisees and claimed they taught that God was an ass. His polemics were too heavy-handed, even for a tolerant age like our own. They proved intolerable in an age of intolerance. Calvinists and Lutherans were eager to prove their basic orthodoxy to the world in opposition to the vagaries of the ecstatic sectarians who also claimed to be reforming the church. Although historically these factors were important, they do not touch the basic issue that separated the liberal Christian humanism of the Renaissance from the Protestant Reformation. The humanistic sectarians were never able to formulate clearly their doctrine of the divinity of Christ. While they rejected the errors of the late medieval theology, they actually rejected far more. They rejected the basic conviction behind the Athanasian Christology. This was belief in Jesus Christ as true God. Salvation cannot come from a uniquely inspired man, nor even from some subordinate form of deity. This conviction, which had been given classic formulation in the patristic age by the Athanasian homoousios formula, was basic to the Reformers. They understood the rejection of Trinitarianism by the left-wing theologians as far more than the rejection of an improper, or non-Biblical, formula. They saw, instead, the rejection of a basic part of the Christian doctrine of salvation. The Reformers were at one with the church of the first ecumenical councils in believing that in Christ, God is fully present and at work for the salvation of man. This conviction was intimately linked in the theology of the Reformation with the doctrine of man as a sinner. It was only as God himself acted directly, the Reformers argued, that man caught in the trammels of original sin could be saved. There was no point at which a divine influence or inspiration could make contact with man to lift him from his fallen estate. Anything less than God himself was unequal to the task. Despite the high honor given Christ by the left-wing theologians, their view of Christ was subordinationist. For them, Jesus was a man through whom the oracles of God were given. His divinity was that of a person uniquely endowed with divine power and wisdom. Such a Christ was sufficient to the task of human salvation as understood by the humanists. In their view there were points of contact by which the ethical and religious instruction of the divinely sent Teacher could lift man to his rightful place. The Reformers may have found fault with the Athanasian terminology, especially in its medieval interpretation, but they eschewed as heresy any Christology that reduced the reality of God in Christ to a subordinate level. The theologians of the left wing sought a middle way between rejection of the divinity of Christ and the acceptance of its Trinitarian form. Their Christology was caught between a yes and a no. As Servetus tried to sum up the matter of Christ's divinity, "Christ is the very image of the substance, or essence of God which has no reference to the divine natures."[17] In saying this he had crossed a divide that was to separate classical Protestantism from the new liberal Christianity.

## The Racovian Catechism

The earliest pioneers of the new Christology worked as individuals isolated from their communities and from fellowship with those of similar views. Political pressure and popular distrust gave them little opportunity to propagate or elaborate their ideas. Although some found fellowship with Anabaptists and spiritualistic sectarians of their time, this was limited. The rationalistic temper and humanistic culture of the anti-Trinitarians estranged them from their more enthusiastic brethren. When, in the middle of the sixteenth century, Poland came under the rule of the unusually tolerant King Sigismund II, a new possibility was opened. He permitted in his realm not only Catholic, Reformed, and Lutheran churches but also the earliest Unitarian church. Centering in Racow, a community of Christians of anti-Trinitarian persuasion, many of them refugees of persecution, founded churches, schools, and printing presses to disseminate their doctrine. In this haven of toleration theological discussion and research could go on to convert what had been the insights and opinions of brilliant individuals into the worship and doctrine of a church. Poland remained a center of the new theology until, in 1658, under the influence of Jesuit leaders, King Johann Kasimir banished these believers. But in scarcely more than a century the insights of the earlier anti-Trinitarians matured into a systematic statement of theology given classical expression in the so-called Racovian Catechism. The catechism, the full title of which is *Catechism of the Churches of Poland, which confess, according to Scripture, one God, the Father, his only begotten Son, and the Holy Spirit,* received its popular title from the Polish city of Racow in which it first appeared. This document was destined to be the most important work in disseminating the new Christology. Servetus' writings dropped into obscurity except for a Dutch translation in 1620, and a reprint, or more accurately a counterfeit edition, made in the eighteenth century. Writings of other anti-Trinitarians were often forced into obscurity by the heresy hunters. It remained for the Racovian Catechism, both its printings in Poland and subsequent editions in Holland, to provide the main thread for relating the beginnings of the new Christology to its full development in the future. The leading intellectual figure behind the catechism was Faustus Socinus, who had fled to Poland from Italy. From him the theology of the catechism received its popular name—Socinianism. However, work on a catechism had started among the Polish Unitarian churches before Socinus arrived. By 1574 a catechism by George Schoman had appeared in Cracow and another by Gregory Paul was also common. Faustus Socinus and Peter Statorius were given the task of revising the various instructional materials. The finished product contained material from the tracts of Socinus, along with the earlier work of the Polish communities, edited into the question-and-answer form of the catechism. This work was not finished before Socinus' death in 1604, when Valentine Smalcius and Jerome Moscorovius were given the task of bringing it to completion. The Polish edition appeared in 1605, followed by a Latin version in 1609.

To apply the title "catechism" to the Racovian Catechism is initially misleading. It does not have the lapidary form of simple, direct assertions usually found in a catechism. It is not a catechism for the instruction of children. It is rather, as Harnack characterized it, "a course of instruction for educating theologians." Socinianism was committed to a theology both Biblical and rational. Yet in the Racovian Catechism the clashes between rationalism and Biblicism are not clearly perceived or resolved. In many respects it remains a product of medieval Catholicism. Its conception of faith is intellectualist. The religion of works and human merits lives on in the catechism. However, the catechism made a basic break with its age. The break was not complete or systematically "modern," but it did provide a challenge to the churches of the Reformation that claimed they had carried through the necessary reforms on the basis of Scripture alone. The Socinians asked a further question: What was the right and importance of the rationalistic, humanistic thought in reforming the church?

The Christology of the Racovian Catechism was to come from the New Testament, interpreted now by rational analysis. The rejection of the traditional interpretation required a detailed, verse-by-verse refutation of the Biblical support given by orthodox theologians for the Trinity and the two-natures doctrine. The fanciful allegory and awkward anachronisms of orthodox exegesis came under the glaring light of philosophical and historical criticism. The exegetical arguments of the catechism became a veritable arsenal for anti-Trinitarians in centuries to come, as they sought to uncover the non-Biblical character of orthodoxy. Constructively, the teachings about Christ are rooted in the doctrine of God. The being of God is interpreted in the light of his sovereignty. But unlike the other great expounder of the divine sovereignty in that day, John Calvin, the Socinians came to Unitarian rather than Trinitarian conclusions. God is defined as "the supreme Lord of all, . . . who, in his own right, has dominion over all things, and is dependent upon no other being in the administration of his government."[18] If the authority of God is truly supreme, it is argued, he must necessarily be one. Authority shared by several persons cannot be supreme because the authority of one person limits that of the others. To speak of three Persons in the Godhead is to speak of a God who is not really supreme.

The Socinians were well aware of the rejoinder that the defenders of Trinitarianism could make. They do not believe in three gods but one. God is one in essence while being three in Persons. Drawing on arguments from Servetus and the early writings of Faustus Socinus himself, the Racovian Catechism rejects the distinction between "essence" and "person" that is so basic to Trinitarianism. A person is "an individual intelligent essence." If there were three persons, there would have to be three essences. This is impossible because "the essence of God is one not in kind but in number." The anti-Trinitarians, as did their nominalistic forebears within the church, defined "person" in individualistic, psychological terms rather than in metaphysical ones as had the patristic theologians. A person is an individual, thinking being. Such a definition reduces Trinitarianism to irrationality. The critical question that the anti-Trinitarians, as well as their opponents, failed to ask was whether their definition of "person" was the same as that of the council fathers who had adopted the terminology in the first place. For better or worse the doctrine of the Trinity was attacked and defended more in the light of its medieval interpretations than of its patristic definition.

The divinity of Christ is described by the catechism in the same fashion as had Servetus. Christ is divine by virtue of his unique share in the divine power. He may rightfully be called God because Scripture uses the term in two ways. Basically, God is the one who is dependent on no one else for his being and power. The term "God" can also be applied to those beings to whom God has given "some kind of superior authority, . . . and is thus rendered in some sense, a partaker of the deity of the one God."[19] The special powers of Christ are not his own possession. They are not his essence because in essence he is a man. Unlike other men, Christ is capable of miracles, holiness, wisdom, and finally resurrection. Yet all of these do not separate him in essence from other men. This Christology is supported by a practical, moral argument. Christ could not be the source of moral instruction and inspiration to men, the catechism teaches, if he was not a real man himself. His resurrection would hold no hope for man's resurrection if it were simply divine immortality asserting itself.

Concern for the practical, moral, and religious meaning of Christ was the heart of the Racovian Catechism. As a church document aimed at guidance in practical rather than speculative matters, it gives large place to the saving work of Christ. The catechism uses the threefold schema of Prophet, Priest, and King, as did the Lutherans and Calvinists. But the emphasis is clearly on the prophetic office. The usual dominance of the priestly office and of sacrificial language is rejected. It is as Prophet that Christ is the mediator of the new covenant, not as Priest. In the brief treatment of the priestly office the language of "expiatory sacrifice" is retained. Such words, it is cautioned, must be taken "by way of similitude" and not literally. It was not Christ's death that made satisfaction but his unswerving obedience to the divine will. The Socinian analysis of the doctrine of substitutionary atonement showed how it went beyond the Biblical materials, drawing on legal theory and medieval practice. The Socinians perceived the doctrinal development that separated the Biblical teachings from orthodox doctrine. They made a discovery abundantly supported by later scholarship, yet one unheeded by their contemporaries.

Stripped of non-Biblical ideas the doctrine of atonement is reduced to one basic truth: the divine forgiveness is free. Mercy is God's eternal character, not something created by the death of Christ. If men had not wandered from God in sin, Christ would not have had to die. His death reveals the love of God in such a way as to call men back to their heavenly Father.

> For Christ delivered himself to death for our sins, in order that he might claim and emancipate us for himself. . . . For by this his great love he turns back to himself those who had gone astray.[20]

The death of Christ not only calls men back to obedience but also gives the highest confirmation of his teachings. Christ taught men to live in love with one another no matter what the

cost. In following his own teachings, Christ met a painful and
ignominious death. In his suffering and death he identifies with
those who were to follow him. He showed that it is possible to
live in obedience to God despite the world's opposition. His
resurrection proves that the life of faith and obedience has a
happy consummation. Eternal life is a reward that far outweighs
the sufferings of this life. The catechism shifts the emphasis from
the death of Christ as a sacrifice. It is Christ as teacher and
martyr who dominates the Socinian doctrine of reconciliation.
Yet he is more. Now in his exalted position at the right hand of
God he makes intercession for us. He may be adored and his
help invoked without fear of idolatry because of his exalted divine status. Still, the believer may identify with the man Jesus
and through him have confidence in approaching God the
Father. Without Christ we could not have such confidence because God is in himself too august and distant. It is the vision of
Christ that keeps men from faltering and falling into despair as
they seek to follow the will of God. Now in his exaltation as
King, victorious over all, Christ gives the believer confidence
that he will be able to deliver him from any power in this
world. It was a vision of Christ suited to a martyr church. The
stringently radical pacifist ethic of some of the Polish Unitarians
brought them into conflict with the state when, in the name
of Christ, they refused to bear arms. Finally they were called to
witness to their faith when their tiny communities were engulfed
in the sea of intolerance sweeping across Europe in the seventeenth century.

The Christology of the Racovian Catechism stands on the
boundary between the medieval and the modern world. Viewed
in one way, the Christ of Socinianism is the enlarged picture of
the medieval saint. He is our example, our inspiration, and
finally our intercessor opening the way to God. He stands with
us in life, as one like us, to illumine the arduous road of sacrifice,
humility, and obedience that leads to the vision of the unap-
proachable and distant God. Viewed in another way, the Christ
of Socinianism is the forerunner of the religion of the Enlightenment. He is the great moral and religious teacher who disen-
tangles from superstition and error the rational truth of Scrip-

ture. He is the example of piety and obedience. In his resurrection he is the verification of his own teaching. Christ is the prophet of the one God, the moral life, and the hope of reward or punishment in a world to come. In Socinianism the old and the new are mixed. It remained for others to disentangle them.

## The Line of Witnesses

No more adequate testimony to the importance of Socinian writings in the seventeenth century is to be found than the polemics of its enemies. In his Christmas sermon, 1665, Robert South warned his fellow Oxonians of a most powerful heresy at work in their midst:

Socinus laid the foundation of that great babel of blasphemies with which he afterwards so amused and pestered the Christian world, and under the colour of reforming and refining the best of religions, has employed the utmost skill and art in bringing men indeed to believe in none.[21]

To the defenders of orthodoxy, Socinianism seemed to be the heresy behind all the new and troubling ideas. Although these estimates of its importance were exaggerated, Socinian writings proved to be the crucial means of bringing the new Christology to the attention of Christendom. By early in the seventeenth century the books and doctrines of Socinianism were known in England, France, Germany, and Holland. Until their suppression, the printing presses of Racow sent out a constant stream of books. Already by 1608 a German translation of the catechism was made. In 1609 an edition was printed with a dedication to James I of England for circulation there, although it should be noted that James did not appreciate the gesture. After the suppression of the Unitarian Church in Poland the work of publication continued in Amsterdam, or Irenopolis, as the Socinians liked to call it. Already by 1597 Socinianism had found a foothold among the Mennonites in Holland. Later the Socinian tracts were widely circulated among the Remonstrant or Arminian churches. This new center for Socinian publications produced many editions of the Racovian Catechism and tracts in convenient pocket size to facilitate smuggling into unwelcome places or for slipping quickly out of the sight of overly zealous onlookers. Through these books the message of Socinianism was heard and pondered by philosophers, theologians, students, ministers, and laymen who never had any direct contact with a Socinian church or pastor. The true missionaries of the new doctrines were the printing presses of Racow and Amsterdam.

A list of the students of Socinianism during the seventeenth century reads like an edition of *Who's Who*. Isaac Newton, John Milton, and John Locke were students of Socinianism. John Biddle (1615–1662), the "father of English Unitarianism," forged out his theology on the basis of Socinianism.[22] Hugo Grotius (1583–1645) had made contact with Socinian refugees from Poland while in Paris and had found in them support and inspiration for his own program of religious modernization. Despite their great influence Socinian writings were still officially banned and burned in Europe. As late as 1654 a translation of the Racovian Catechism was burned by the hangman of London. Yet the underground traffic continued unabated. Theologians rose to refute what the state did not suppress. In 1613 the University of Wittenberg brought out an official refutation of Socinianism. The Lutheran orthodox theologian Abraham Calovius refuted the heresy at length, and a host of Dutch Calvinists—Johannes Hoornbeek, Samuel Maresius, *et al.*— poured out their polemics. Their work was soon echoed by English writers and preachers, particularly the Calvinists. Much of this polemic literature was simply a catalog of the teachings of Socinianism and how they differed from church confessions, and so by definition of the orthodox, from Scripture. The exegetical arguments of the catechism were supposedly refuted by the orthodox writers. But the issue remained unclear. The opponents seemed to speak past one another. Socinians sought support for their interpretations by rationalistic, philological, and historical analysis. The orthodox seldom dealt directly with these arguments. They repeated their own interpretation of Scripture made upon what they took to be the only proper basis of exegesis, the confessional position of the church. Here were two opposing approaches, not only to Scripture but toward religion itself. Francis Cheynell, the English polemicist, saw the issue more clearly than did most of his contemporaries in *The Rise, Growth, and Danger of Socinianism,* 1643. According to Cheynell, the issue at stake was that of revelation and reason. The belief that reason can discover and verify the truths of religion is the foundation principle of Socinianism. Unfettered reason stands behind the heresies of Socinus. Only as this is perceived and rejected can the dangers of Socinianism be escaped. The mediating theologian who seeks some middle ground between reason and revelation is left to fight a losing battle—trying to defend the faith yet losing one crucial doctrine after the other to omnivorous reason. The truth of Cheynell's estimate of the situation was to become only too clear in the centuries ahead. There was a new principle at work in Socinian theology. It was the principle of autonomous reason that no longer measured its limits by revelation. Rather, reason was to measure the limits of revelation.

*Chapter III*

# CHRIST

# AND THE

# NEW WORLD OF MAN

*The Next Step*

The evolution of modernity and its unique religious conscious-ness cannot be understood solely in the light of the humanistic spirit of the Renaissance. New elements had to come into the arena of thought from the understanding of the world given by science. During the seventeenth century the astronomy and physics that had started to develop in the previous centuries pro-duced an integrated picture of the universe in the work of Newton. The age of exploration was well under way, bringing to Western European man an ever-growing awareness of other cultures and religions. Human geography was revolutionized. The easy parochialism that assumed Christianity to be the only religion, or that its claim to revelation was unique, was crum-bling. Religious questions were destined in this new age to be thought out in a larger context. The significance of Jesus could not be verified by church dogma or Scripture. His claims had to be adjudicated before the reason of men newly aware of their own powers and of the complexity of the world in which they lived. The possibility of revelation had to be rethought in rela-tion to the world view that had pushed God to the edge of reality. The Copernican revolution was not simply the shift from a geocentric to a heliocentric universe. More deeply the new astronomy presaged the shift from a theocentric to an anthro-pocentric consciousness in Western man.

In England in the late seventeenth and early eighteenth centuries modern science and philosophy came into decisive and creative relation with religious thought. John Locke and the deists unfolded a new Christology in part reflecting, and in part creating, the new religious situation of the time. To grasp the complex of forces at work it is necessary to trace not only the influence of Socinianism but also the theological situation of seventeenth-century England. These were the building blocks out of which men tried to build a bridge between Christian faith and the new world of science.

## Socinianism and the English Theology

In the seventeenth century few people would gladly own to the name "Socinian." Most writers in this early liberal tradition preferred the name "Unitarian" or even "Anti-Trinitarian," admitting the term "Socinian" only as a popular designation. In 1684, Christopher Sandius entitled his study of the new theology *Bibliotheca Anti-Trinitariorum,* to which he appended a history of the Unitarian Church, *qui Sociniani vulge audient.* Even John Locke was reluctant to admit to the influence of Socinian ideas on his religious thought despite the considerable evidence of its presence.[1] Hugo Grotius wrote a *Defence of the Catholic Faith Concerning the Satisfaction of Christ Against Faustus Socinus.* Yet by the end of the century, a historian could refer to Grotius as being "right well socinianized." The reluctance of many who shared Socinian ideas to accept the name, let alone admit to an uncritical dependence on its theology, was, in part, an unwillingness to have their ideas stigmatized by association with an unpopular cause. They feared guilt by association. In addition, there was an uncertainty among many early liberal theologians about the adequacy of Socinianism. In his *Defence,* Grotius was trying to overcome the lopsided moralism of Socinian teaching on the atonement by emphasizing the priority of divine forgiveness. Then as now there was a deep cleft between finding new insights in a theology and claiming it uncritically as one's own. But even more basic, Socinianism was not the only source of the new rationalistic-Biblicistic ways of thinking. In England there had developed since the Reformation a theological climate far more open to the rationalistic temper of the day than were the orthodoxies that dominated Lutheran and Reformed churches on the Continent. The religious liberals of the late seventeenth century could as well look to this tradition as the ground and inspiration of their theology as to the direct impact of Socinianism.

Richard Hooker (1554–1600) reflects the spirit of Anglican theology in his *Laws of Ecclesiastical Polity*. The influence of the humanistic reformation envisaged by More and Colet was far from overwhelmed by Calvinism in the theology of "the judicious Mr. Hooker." For Hooker the ultimate tests of religious truth were conscience and reason. In matters of religion he did not believe authority "should prevail with men either against or above reason."[2] By no stretch of the imagination could Hooker's theology be thought of as being tainted with Socinianism. His results were always eminently orthodox. But what was important was his development of a theology that gave such large place to reason in determining the extent and meaning of revelation. Man could not know or worship God "but for the light of natural reason that shineth in him, and maketh him apt to apprehend the things of God." Such a theological climate allowed the development of a modern Christology in England long before it could penetrate the intricate but closed systems of Protestant orthodoxy that denied reason a role in apprehending revelation. The Anglicans of the tumultuous seventeenth century carried this mediating rationalism and Biblicism as a hallmark in distinction to their Presbyterian opponents. Archbishop Laud, the very prototype of high-church authoritarianism, was able to write, "For though I set the mysteries of faith above reason, which is their proper place; yet I would have no man think they contradict reason, or the principles thereof."[3] High views of churchly authority did not exclude a respect for the power of human reason in matters of religion. Francis Cheynell, one of Laud's Calvinist critics, was quick to point out that such concessions to reason lead inevitably to heresy. According to Cheynell, to be so accepting of reason is tantamount to being soft on Socinianism.[4] Yet one could name a whole host of English theologians in this tradition of moderate rationalism who remained sound churchmen in no sense compromised by heresy. Despite the warnings of their Calvinistic critics as to the danger of their position, seventeenth-century Anglicans believed that their moderate rationalism could comfortably support "the orthodoxy of the Bible and the councils of the undivided church." This confidence was to be sorely tested and greatly chastened in the storms of deistic controversy that were as yet tiny clouds on the horizon.

## *Natural Religion*

Alongside this moderate Anglicanism there developed a new form of religious thought that held there was a sufficient ground within human reason alone for knowing God and finding eternal felicity in fulfilling his will. Edward, Lord Herbert of Cherbury (1583–1648), in his *De Veritate,* 1624, sought to establish a religious system without specific reference to revelation or to the authority of church or Scripture. His starting point was not new. The root idea of a knowledge of God and morality given to men by virtue of their reason and conscience goes back into classical Christian thought. The theologians of Protestant orthodoxy had maintained that this knowledge of God and human duty was, paradoxically, great enough to justify God's condemnation of man, but not enough to ensure human salvation. The saving truth could come from revelation alone. In Lord Herbert, natural theology was given a new form. Instead of being a tiny vestibule to the greater structure of revelation, natural religion was to be a house complete in itself.

*De Veritate* was not primarily a theological work, although it was its theology that provided its claim to fame. Basically the book is an investigation of human knowledge, its possibilities and limitations. According to Lord Herbert, man has been given certain basic "natural instincts" by God in his creation. These natural instincts provide man with a means of knowing a number of "common notions." The common notions are innate and comprise "that part of knowledge with which we are endowed in the primeval plan of nature."[5] These common notions are innate in man; hence, they are universal in scope, being found in all men. The common notions represent the core of certainty given to man by his rational powers or natural instincts. By finding the common notions in religion it would be possible to determine the universally valid core of truth in the various religions. Lord Herbert holds there are five basic religious dogmas dictated by the natural instincts: belief in one supreme God; the worship of God with a piety expressed through virtue; God's commandments to men to live a holy life; the call of men to repentance when they fail in moral obedience; and finally, the reward or punishment of men for their moral life in a life after death.[6] "The only Catholic and uniform Church is the doctrine of the common notions which comprehends all places and men. This Church alone reveals Divine Universal Providence, or the wisdom of Nature."[7] Any church that claims efficacy for its special doctrines is not catholic despite its most vehement claims. It is schismatic from the true church of humanity.

"The wisdom of Nature" which God has given man is the key to the necessary truth in religion. Revelation is possible but only as an alternative way of delivering the truths already available in nature. Certainty can be found only when it is clear that a revelation is in conformity with the common notions. Lord Herbert's analysis of the Ten Commandments concludes: "It is of no importance whether sacred priests or legislators promulgated these laws. . . . They are common notions."[8]

Natural religion promised a way out of the chaos of competing religious absolutisms that racked not only the spiritual life of Europe but also its social and political existence. The period after the Reformation was marked not only by the division between the newly emergent Protestantism and Catholicism but also by the growing fragmentation of Protestantism itself. These divisions were never simply theological but also political, creating on the Continent the chaos of warring confessional states and in England revolutionary struggles. This chaos stemmed from political, social, or economic grounds, yet to the men of the times the issues of doctrinal differences, each shade of opinion claiming infallibility for itself alone, were dominant. Lord Herbert spoke of "this shapeless and monstrous chaos of beliefs" and reflected sadly: "The multitude of sects, divisions, sub-divisions and cross divisions in the schools hope-lessly distracts the wits of the learned and the conscience of the unlettered. Where can an anxious and divided mind turn to find security and peace?"[9] Lord Herbert answered his own question. There is some "spirit of truth" which pervaded this chaos. This is man's God-given ability to know the truth by the use of his own rational powers.

Lord Herbert lived in a day when religious polemics were vivid and vituperative. Although such polemics avoided the polite boredom in which we all try to see the good in someone else's position, they did little to clarify the issues. Orthodox the-ologians warned on every side that Lord Herbert's religious naturalism, or deism as it quickly became known, was nothing but thinly veiled atheism. Orthodox teachers held that the least deviation from a dogmatic system led directly and immediately to atheism. The Cambridge Calvinist John Edwards was able to argue with high seriousness that disbelief in demons or evil spirits was but the first step on a road that led inevitably to atheism. The possibility of critical discernment was denied. The possibility of a creative discussion of the issues raised by Lord Herbert was subverted in orthodox quarters by a rigid dogma-tism. He was a "naturalist" or "atheist," and that was the end of it.

The resistance to Lord Herbert was not simply that of a reac-tionary orthodoxy. The philosophical basis of the common no-tions of natural religion came under withering attack by empiri-cists. Locke, in *An Essay Concerning Human Understanding,* sought to remove Lord Herbert's errors, root and branch. Locke rightfully questioned the universality of the supposedly innate notions of natural religion. The claim that the common notions are universal because they are innate simply did not hold up to critical investigation. The grounds of a natural religion had to be sought elsewhere, according to the empiricists. However, the Lockean critique was not meant to reject the claims of human reason in matters of religion. Instead, its aim was to determine more accurately the basis and scope of reason.

Lord Herbert was very much a prophet crying in the wilder-ness. He did not immediately sway large numbers of people. His philosophical critics were right at many points. His common notions were not so common as he thought. But his cry was a prophetic one destined to dominate religious thinking to the end of the eighteenth century and to appear in various guises ever since. He had struck a basic motif in the religious consciousness of modern man. No matter how men differed as to the extent of natural religion, or argued over its metaphysical basis, one fact remained clear. Natural religion, the religion known by man through his own capabilities, was to be the crucial criterion in forming the new image of Christ.

## *Theology and Physics*

Often the impact of the new scientific world view has been measured in terms of the destruction of the mythological cosmology of Scripture or of the ancient theologians. The absurdity and the intransigence of churchmen, not only in the seventeenth century but later, on everything from the movement of comets to the age of fossils, have given credence to such an overly simple view of the relation of science to religion. Churchmen defending untenable positions on astronomy, physics, geology, and biology, supposedly on the authority of Scripture, were constantly forced to retract their theology when authoritarianism could no longer stem the tide of scientific truth. Such are the terms of the drama as unfolded in White's *The Warfare of Science with Religion.* The conflict was thought of in terms of the contradiction between particular dogmas of religion and the discoveries of science. But the issues are more subtle and complex than such a rendering of the question indicates. To paint the reaction of Christian thought to science purely in terms of negativism is to misunderstand the growth of the new picture of Christ. By the end of the seventeenth century some religious thinkers had started to investigate the positive implications of scientific knowledge for theology.

To understand the relationship of Christian faith to the new world of science it is necessary to look to the underlying changes that science produced in man's consciousness of himself, his world, and his power. Men had come to understand their place in the created order in the light of a cosmology fashioned in the

Middle Ages by combining a Christianized version of the Aristotelian physics with the astronomy and geography of Claudius Ptolemaeus. This picture had gathered great authority about it by the fifteenth century. It was thought to be supported by Scripture. It was backed by the church and by the best philosophical minds. It had great advantage in being able to combine the extant science with the comprehensive picture of God and human destiny given by Christian faith. Christian theology had developed in such close relation to this world view that it was easy to assume it was a part of revelation itself. Certainly the Bible gives evidence of a geocentric world view. How else, men argued, could you make sense of Joshua's great miracle of making the sun stand still during a battle?

When the major steps by which classical physics and astronomy emerged are viewed from a purely logical standpoint, it is difficult to see why they created problems for theology. The essential discoveries can be simply stated in outline:

1. Copernicus' discovery that the earth moves around the sun, and not the sun around the earth.
2. Kepler's description of the planetary paths as elliptical.
3. Galileo's discovery of the laws of motion or inertia.
4. Newton's discovery of the law of gravitation and the integration of the picture of the universe on a mathematical basis through the use of calculus.

There are no logically necessary theological implications in these statements. They are simply more adequate interpretations of the physical world. Logically, there is nothing more inimical to God and spiritual reality in Kepler's ellipses than in Ptolemy's epicycles. As was soon perceived, the clashes with the Biblical cosmology could be handled through understanding the essentially poetic nature of the Biblical descriptions of the universe. A simple expedient would be to separate theological ideas from ideas about the physical world; this was the expedient to which theology was finally driven. But the acceptance of such a separation was neither simple nor immediate. Christian theology had developed in the Middle Ages and in the Reformation within a comprehensive picture of reality that integrated man's understanding of the created order with his knowledge of God. There were deeper reasons for supporting the old world view than the widely held belief that the authority of the Bible was behind it. Far more important, the Aristotelian-Ptolemaic picture of the world provided a way of explaining how God is related to the world, which the new science excluded. The most basic arguments of the theologians against the new science were primarily philosophical rather than Biblical. How is it possible to say that God acts within the world in revelation and redemption? The Aristotelian-Ptolemaic system provided a cogent answer to this question which modern science threatened to undo. Philipp Melanchthon gave great attention to the teaching of physics as a basis for theology. A knowledge of God's world was a presupposition of the knowledge of how God redeemed the world. In his *Initia doctrinae physicae,* 1549, Melanchthon defended the Aristotelian-Ptolemaic system against the Copernican hypothesis. His refutation took the form of a philosophical argument. He saw the new scientific views as the recrudescence of the ancient errors of the atomists Lucretius, Epicurus, and Democritus. The question at issue was how to conceive the order of the world. The Christianized Aristotelianism of scholasticism, both Catholic and Protestant, held that the order of the cosmos is not inherent in the cosmos itself. Taken out of its relation to God, the cosmos is the realm of unformed matter. God is the spiritual ground and goal of the whole cosmos. The orderliness and meaning of the cosmos are the product of its relation to God. God and supernatural beings act as causal agents in the universe. The world is not a closed system kept running according to its own laws. Rather, the realm of secondary causes—the realm explored by science—is dependent upon the First Cause.

The ancient atomists, like the modern scientists, believed the order of the universe to be inherent in the universe itself. The atomistic philosophers of classical antiquity believed that the order of the world was the result of the movements of the atoms. These movements are not determined by the relation of the cosmos to God. Meaning and order must be understood in terms of the atoms themselves. Such a system provided no means of conceiving how God can act in the world. The world is a closed system explained in terms of this-worldly realities.

Melanchthon saw the new scientific theories as an attempt to explain the world order in terms of causalities within the universe instead of by its relation to God. Any system of thought moving in this direction is moving down the road to materialism and atheism. Melanchthon rightly perceived that a God left standing on the edge of the world is but one step removed from no God at all. He believed that God could not be excluded from any part of reality. How else can God be Lord save as he sustains the natural world and reveals himself in miracles? Scholastic philosophy provided a means of making such a faith in God intelligible. To turn away from this and fall back into the oft-refuted errors of the ancient atomists was to be precipitated into a problem from which no escape seemed possible.

When we turn to the writings of the philosophers and scientists whose work had done most to undermine the world view of medieval Christianity, the forebodings of the theologians seem ill-founded. The scornful agnosticism of the eighteenth-century Encyclopedists had little part in the work of the great pioneers of the sixteenth and seventeenth centuries. Many were men of deep piety, greatly concerned with theology. An important possibility for relating science and theology was created by the philosophy of René Descartes (1596–1650). The Cartesian philosophy was the first modern philosophy to attain systematic expression and wide influence. It provided an alternative to the Aristotelian Scholasticism of the Middle Ages as a structure for integrating thought. Descartes's philosophy envisaged a dualism between the realm of extension, i.e., physical bodies, and the realm of thought which included the reality of the spiritual. By such a distinction it is possible to give the physical sciences a free rein to investigate nature, while theology and philosophy have the possibility of reflecting on man and his relation to God. There was to be a separation between natural and religious knowledge. Each had its own proper sphere. Such a distinction had already been drawn by some of the nominalistic philosophers and was congenial to many churchmen. The Catholic theologian Nicholas de Malebranche (1638–1715) followed in this tradition, sharpening the distinction between scientific knowledge and faith. Such a dualism offered a way of accepting the new scientific knowledge without disturbing the realm of thought traditionally treated by theology. A kind of eclectic Cartesianism influenced much Roman Catholic theology during the early modern period, although it was often viewed with suspicion.

The dangers and difficulties that attended this Cartesian dualism soon became apparent. It greatly restricted the realm of religious knowledge and threatened to separate it into the sphere of irrational opinion supported only by ecclesiastical authority. Such was not to the liking of the English philosophical interpreters of science. English theology in this period remained wary of Cartesian dualism in the interest of investigating more fully the possibility of theology developed in relation to the new science. The outlook of these scientists and philosophers was well summed up in the title of a book by Robert Boyle (1627–1691), *The Christian Virtuoso, Shewing that by being addicted to Experimental Philosophy, a Man is rather assisted than indisposed to be a good Christian*. His aim was to develop a physicotheology, i.e., a theology in direct continuity with the results of the physical sciences rather than in isolation from them. Such was the hope of these scientists. It is asserted again and again in their writings like an article of faith. But it proved to be an ideal far more difficult in fulfilling than in conceiving.

## *Newton and the Spacious Firmament on High*

Towering above the scientists and philosophers of the seventeenth century in England stands Isaac Newton (1642–1727). He not only fulfilled the role of creative scientist but was also the synthesizer and philosopher interpreting the meaning of the astronomy and physics that had developed since Copernicus. Like his scientific contemporaries, Newton was greatly concerned with theology, ranging in his thinking from the doctrine of God to commentaries on Daniel and Revelation. Referring to his *Principia* in a letter to Richard Bentley, Newton wrote: "When I wrote my treatise about our system, I had an eye on such principles as might work with considering men for the belief of a Deity; and nothing can rejoice me more than to find it useful for that purpose."[10] Newton hoped that as knowledge of physics—natural philosophy—grew, so would moral philosophy. As natural philosophy clarified "what is the first Cause, what Power he has over us, and what Benefits we receive from him, so far our Duty towards him, as well as that towards one another, will appear to us by the Light of Nature."[11] As science rids men of superstition and idolatry that "had blinded the Heathen," they can learn to worship God aright through moral obedience. Such noble intentions should serve to allay the fears of any but the most crabbed theologians. Yet charges of materialism and incipient atheism were sounded from pulpit and lecture hall. The universe according to Newton was a closed system, a perfect clockwork mechanism, his critics argued. Indeed, Newton himself said the world was controlled by "the Laws of Nature," and "once form'd it may continue by these Laws for many ages."[12] How can God be Lord of such a world order? Where could the miracles of revelation and redemption take place? It is true Newton celebrated God as the Creator of this perfect universe. He believed it "unphilosophical," or perhaps as we would say today, "unscientific," to maintain that the world "might arise out of a chaos by the mere Laws of Nature." To put God at the beginning of the world as its architect was not enough if he were not also sustaining the world. Christian faith is not only faith in a Creator but in the Lord of history and the Redeemer of men.

Newton's critics had jumped to conclusions from which he personally drew back. While unambiguously celebrating the rationality and order of the universe, Newton did not believe the order to be absolutely perfect. Irregularities "which may have arisen from the mutual actions of Comets and Planets upon one another," would continue to increase "till this System wants a Reformation."[13] How else, save by the direct action of God, Newton argued, was it possible to explain why other solar systems revolving around the fixed stars did not collide into our own? God was the great clockmaker, to be sure, but, as Leibniz once quipped, in Newton's system he was "a most unskillful workman," unable to make "a perfect machine at the beginning but was under the necessity of tinkering with it from time to time." Yet attributing to God these housekeeping functions eventually proved to be as unwarranted scientifically as inadequate theologically. It simply did not answer the question of the Lordship of God. Newton grasped the Biblical faith in the Lordship of God while struggling in terms of his world system to give it intellectual meaning.

> This Being governs all things, not as the soul of the world, but as Lord over all; and on account of his dominion he is wont to be called *Lord God pantokrator,* or Universal Ruler; for God is a relative word, and has a respect to servants; and Deity is the dominion of God not over his own body, as those imagine who fancy God to be the soul of the world, but over servants.[14]

The Lord God is omnipresent in the world. Infinite space is the sensorium of God in which he "sees the things themselves intimately, and thoroughly perceives them, and comprehends them wholly by their immediate presence to himself."[15] The paradox of Newton's position becomes evident when he faces the all-important question of how God effects his Lordship over the world.

> In him are all things contained and moved; yet neither affects the other: God suffers nothing from the motion of bodies; bodies find no resistance from the omnipresence of God.[16]

God is present to see and know all. But it is impossible to say that he shapes any particular event. God cannot be introduced as a causal agent into the universe because events can be fully explained in terms of their natural causalities. As Newton himself said, "We are to admit no more causes of natural things than such as are both true and sufficient to explain their appearances."[17] The natural causes are the "true and sufficient" ones.

This is not to question the depth and seriousness of Newton's religious concerns. Although his Christology was adjudged Arian from the perspective of a rigid orthodoxy, he was not seeking to be a doctrinal innovator or self-styled radical. Newton's religion developed in the English tradition of a moderate rationalistic Biblicism. His demurrers about the Trinity, the preexistence of Christ, or the consubstantiality of the Son were not concessions he made to modernity but the result of what he took to be a more accurate reading of Scripture than that of the Nicene and Chalcedonian orthodoxy. He sought to be a defender of the faith in the new world of science. He understood the importance of the Biblical assertions of the sovereignty of God. But he was unable to find a way of integrating this faith into his understanding of the universe. He could relate God to the breaks and gaps in his mechanistic system, but such concessions fell far short of his espousal of the Universal Ruler. Yet there remained one other factor of basic importance for Newton's religious thought. Alongside what can be said about God in nature, there is God's activity in the realm of grace, in his self-revelation through Christ as witnessed to in Scripture. "Newton evidently cherished a kind of religious experience, nourished largely, of course, by tradition, that was in the main detachable from the theism postulated as a corollary to science."[18] The authority of the Bible and a traditional Christian faith were great for Newton. However, he does not clarify how these ideas relate to his general world view. God's gracious care of mankind is a matter of sufficient gravity to allow the great architect to take exception to the rules of his universe. The miracles that are impossible from the standpoint of nature become actual because of God's grace in calling men back to himself. Theoretical difficulties did not overthrow the authority of a religious tradition as powerful as that of Christianity in seventeenth-century England.

Newton's interpretation of the meaning of the new science for religion was the dominant one in the seventeenth century. At the same time there was a minority opinion far more radical in its implications for theology. Yet it was an opinion never clearly heard or accepted by the men of that day. Baruch Spinoza (1632–1677) followed the inner logic of the mechanistic view of the world to its conclusion. For him it was more than mechanistic explanation; it was a vision of God in the world. If the web of causal relationships was all-embracing, as the new science taught, then there could be no gaps or exceptions. In the light of such a vision of the world the focal point of religion had shifted. It was not in the direct, personal, daily intervention of God in the natural order to overcome its deficiencies. Nor was it in the miraculous events by which God carried out human salvation. Rather, it was in contemplation of God as Creator of a perfect universe. Its miraculous perfection replaced faith in the particular miracles through which men once believed they had seen God's redemptive intervention.

As everything is true with necessity only according to divine decision, it follows perfectly clearly that the general laws of nature are merely God's decisions, which follow from the necessity and perfection of the divine nature. If therefore something should happen in nature that is in contradiction to its general laws, it would also be in contradiction to the decision, reason, and nature of God, or if someone wished to maintain that God acted against the laws of nature, he would also have to maintain that He acted against His own nature, which is perfectly absurd.[19]

In Spinoza's scheme a miracle is not the revelation of God but the denial of God, for the will of God is identical with the laws of nature. God is not to be fitted into the gaps in our scientific knowledge because in principle there are no gaps. Nor can God exist in some supernatural realm set apart from the universe, for no such realm can exist.

Theologians were quick to decry Spinoza's conception of God as *Deus sive natura* as, at best, pantheism and, at worst, atheism. Even the philosophers and scientists rejected Spinoza. Among the theologians it was only the brilliant but little-known Dutch Calvinist Christoph Wittich (1625–1687) who recognized both the challenge and the creative possibilities in Spinoza's metaphysics.[20] Wittich perceived the danger for modern theology in making God over in all too human terms. Theology produces intellectual idols (*idolum cerebri mei*) because it proceeds falsely through the misuse of analogical arguments to discover the nature of God. The relationship between God and man is not simply that between great and small. Rather, the relationship is that between the imperfect and the perfect, between a being bound by time and one free of time. God is not simply amplified man. Such a critique could have been of great value for the theology developing in England at this time. For as the new understanding of the universe was causing theology to speak of God more and more as the great builder or architect of "the world machine," it produced a set of problems for the doctrine of God from which there was no escape. In the Newtonian scheme God had created a world in which he had no real or abiding place. Theology was left constantly looking for some way to fit God into the picture. Wittich, drawing on Spinoza's analysis, saw the root of this problem in the all too human picture of God as the great artificer, creating something that stands in contradiction to him. In good Calvinistic fashion, rejecting Spinoza's tendency to identify God with nature, Wittich believed Spinoza was right in asserting that freedom and necessity, will and fulfillment, are one in God. This constitutes the divine perfection. The world as the result of God's will does not stand in contradiction to God's being. Creation has always been part of God's will, even though from our human standpoint it may be said to have occurred at a point in time. The created order is not a novelty thrust upon God, but is an expression of what God is in himself. There can be no real separation of secondary causes from God the Primary Cause. The same will is found in both.

No matter how important Spinoza or Wittich could have been for the emerging theology of the seventeenth century, their influence was not felt. The patterns were too well set by the end of the century to allow much experimentation with a radical alternative. The new scientifically oriented theology was committed to a vision of God as creator of the wondrous universe it had come to know. Beyond this the theologians saw God at work in the gaps and blind spots of the created order. They looked for God in the miracles, the exceptions to the rules, where to rescue sinful man he was forced to intervene. The precariousness of such a theology was soon to become evident.

*Chapter IV*

# JESUS

# THE MESSIAH

## Empiricism and Religion

The new forces at work reshaping the religion of Western man in the seventeenth century were brought to focus in the mind of John Locke (1632–1704). Locke the philosopher of the new empirical science or the theoretician of democracy is a well-known figure in the history of thought. Locke the theologian and Biblical scholar has often been left as an aside. A present-day reader turning to *The Reasonableness of Christianity as Delivered in the Scriptures* or *An Essay of the Understanding of St. Paul's Epistles* will be in a quandary as to why they raised such a storm of controversy. They are anything but slick in style or polemic in tone. Being a firm believer in the proverb, "A soft answer turneth away wrath," Locke is strangely silent or vague on crucial points. This seeming blandness cannot obscure his epoch-making work. Locke caught the spirit of the age, reflecting the diverse traditions at work in religion, yet providing a new synthesis. Despite his qualms about the term "Socinian," he stands in that tradition of humanistic Christianity reaching back through the Socinians to Erasmus and the Renaissance. Without its vision of man Locke's work would not have been possible. He was also a rightful heir, albeit left of center, to the heritage of rationalistic Biblicism that flows in Anglicanism from Hooker through the Cambridge Platonists and Chillingworth. His theology reflects concern with the ecclesiastical and political exigencies of the day. He may be counted a Latitudinarian seeking an irenic theology to end confessional rivalries. Such a creed Locke sought by his proposal to reduce Christian doctrine to one formula—Jesus is the Messiah.

Both as philosopher and as theologian Locke was concerned about the meaning of the new vitalities let loose by modern science. He had looked deeply into Newton's natural philosophy and pondered its meaning for the religious life. What are the grounds and how wide the scope of faith in the newly described world of science? Content with no Cartesian dualism, Locke would put Christian faith on a rational basis, not by isolating but by integrating it into the truth of science. Like Newton, Locke saw the goodness of God in the works of nature. But this is a kind of anteroom; the crucial revelation of God is in the fulfillment of his gracious promises for the salvation of mankind. "The works of nature show his wisdom and power; but it is his peculiar care of mankind most eminently discovered in his promises to them, that shows his bounty and goodness, and consequently engages their hearts in love and affection to him."[1] Locke wanted to apply the method so successful in the sciences to this inner realm of theology. The basis of the new scientific method was empiricism. Locke's empiricism is not simply more attention to observation or the accumulation of experimental detail. The success of science, he saw, was in relating data to one another by a rational scheme. He gives full place to reason in its proper role—the analysis of experience. Reason cannot spin a web of meaning out of itself. Its task is to clarify relationships within experience and to make inferences about other experiences. Such an empiricism means the rejection of speculation as a guide to truth. By rejecting speculation Locke undercut a major source for elaboration of Christian doctrine. He skirts clear around the doctrine of the Trinity and the two natures of Christ. The inscrutable mysteries of hypostasis and person, nature and substance, are left in the oblivion of problems unsolved because insoluble. Locke was heeding a warning Newton had made to scientists against theories for which there is no observable data. Such theories or doctrines Newton called "hypotheses." In Book III of the *Principia*, he gave his dictum:

"I frame no hypotheses; for whatever is not deduced from the phenomena is to be called an hypothesis; and hypotheses, whether metaphysical or physical, whether of occult qualities or mechanical, have no place in experimental philosophy." His principle has dominated modern scientific philosophy. To transpose this principle into theology, Locke believed, was to lay aside the very matters rendering faith problematic to modern man. It is to the data of experience men must turn for meaning in religion, not to arcane speculation, even when given authority by the church.

Locke rejected a natural religion built on innate ideas, after the style of Lord Herbert. The true starting point for a natural religion is not in reason spinning ideas out of itself but in analyzing experience to find where God makes himself known. The scrutiny of human experience shows two aspects: sensation or experience of the outer world, and reflection or experience of our own inner world of thought. Reflection points beyond itself to God. Through reflection "we have an intuitive knowledge of our own existence, and an internal infallible perception that we are."[2] This "infallible perception that we are" raises a question. What is the source of our own being? Is it possible that man could exist as a thinking being if he did not have his source in an eternal, thinking Being? For Locke the answer is a clear no. For him and his contemporaries it is axiomatic that being cannot come out of nothingness, nor can thinking have its source in anything that is not thought. Since man knows his own existence and can experience his own thought, he can certainly conclude there is a God "eternal, most powerful, and most knowing."[3] Locke would deny that this conclusion is a· speculation. Our own most certain knowledge of ourselves has implicit within it knowledge of God, our Source, without whom our existence would be unthinkable. To an age as yet untouched by the doctrines of naturalistic evolution, the findings of physiological psychology, or the sophistication of computers, such an argument was convincing.

Religion needs building blocks other than knowledge of God. It is also built on knowledge of the moral law. Such knowledge is possible for men because moral laws are rational in their basis. Locke admittedly had problems in trying to educe the rational basis for the radical ethic enjoined by the Gospels. While he is unfailing in his assertion of the rationality of ethics, his arguments to support them have less than perfect clarity. He is convinced that the commandment for love of neighbor and the Golden Rule are rational. Coupled with knowledge of moral law is the freedom of man to fulfill it. But many men do not have a true knowledge of God or his will. Some are polytheists or even atheists. Others follow religions that substitute immoral and absurd rites for morality. Man has fallen from the ethical monotheism for which his nature suits him. This fall is the reason the world needs the Christian message of salvation. The usual church doctrine of the Fall misunderstands what Scripture is really teaching. The doctrine of the Fall brings together two ideas that Locke wishes to separate. First, Adam's fall brought all men under the penalty of death. Second, the Fall brought all men into guilt and bondage. Locke accepts the first assertion, "In Adam all die." But the notion that the Fall implies personal guilt for anyone but Adam, or produces a bondage of the will, Locke rejects as unworthy of a just God. When Scripture says, "In Adam all die" (I Cor. 15:22), death means "a ceasing to be, the losing of all action of life and sense." It does not mean, "Thou and thy posterity shall be, ever after, incapable of doing anything, but what shall be sinful and provoking to me, and shall justly deserve my wrath and indignation."[4] As offspring of Adam we share his loss of immortality. But the only sins of which we are guilty are those we have committed.

Having rejected the notion of the Fall as bondage of the will, Locke still must deal with a fact the traditional doctrine of the Fall explains: Why is mankind caught in this endless welter of immorality, superstition, and idolatry? If the knowledge of the one God and his will is given by reason, and men are free to respond, why do they persist in the irrational course of disobedience leading to eternal punishment? In place of the usual theological explanation, Locke places a psychological and sociological one. He advances a thesis from Lord Herbert, destined to appear repeatedly in rationalistic theologians. Man is a victim of an alliance between oppressive political power and a superstitious priesthood that dulls moral sense with ritual acts of forgiveness and confuses the mind by outlawing the use of reason in religion. Men remain in sin not only because of this conspiracy but also because of the inherent weakness of reason. There have been great philosophers and moralists who possessed "a clear knowledge of God and of their duty." However, looking over the whole course of human history, Locke concludes, "But natural religion, in its full extent, was no-where, that I know, taken care of, by the force of natural reason."[5] Most men are caught in the web of early training and through sloth or lack of rational powers are unable to uncover the truth which is rightfully theirs. "Our Savior found mankind under a corruption of manners and principles, which ages after ages had prevailed, and must be confessed, was not in a way or tendency to be mended."[6]

What hope is there for man to be restored to the immortality and bliss for which God created him? Restoration can come only from a Savior. Without divine intervention man cannot break the hold of ignorance. This Savior is Jesus the Messiah who brings true knowledge of God and his will. As Savior, Jesus brings more than knowledge; he provides a means for justifying all who repent and strive for moral obedience. This "sum of saving knowledge," Locke argues, can be found in one affirmation: "Jesus is the Messiah." Here are no intellectual conundrums to bewilder the mind of the simple, or irrationalities to vex the mind of the wise. This is the doctrine of no party or sect. Rather, it is the unifying faith of the New Testament discovered by empirical study of the documents.

## The Life and Work of Jesus

Locke explores his basic creed—Jesus is the Messiah—in the preaching of Jesus and the apostles. He has no difficulty in supporting his thesis in the preaching in The Acts. But the life of Jesus poses problems. Why is there a guardedness or vagueness in Jesus' preaching on a subject so central? At times, Jesus clearly declared himself Messiah; yet, at other times, he spoke "by phrases and circumlocutions, that did signify or intimate his coming; though not in direct words pointing to his person."[7] Jesus' vagueness or even silence was tactical, Locke concludes. An open declaration of his Messiahship in Jewish public life would have brought the intervention of the Sanhedrin, as a declaration of kingship would have brought the Romans. Jesus had compassion for his people in their bondage and did not want to stir up "the more heady Jews" to a tragically hopeless rebellion. Jesus could have made open proclamation of himself in all places if he chose, and wherever he was endangered, either by Romans or Jews, he could have been given miraculous deliverance as he was at the synagogue in Nazareth. To make such prodigal use of miracles would only create confusion and render his teachings less believable. "If it were not so, the course and evidence of things would be confounded, miracles would lose their name and force; and there could be no distinction between natural and supernatural."[8]

Locke is bothered by the radical ethic of Jesus. If the ethic of Jesus is rational, how can his seemingly unreasonable demands be explained? In the story of the rich young man who comes to Jesus seeking salvation, Jesus tells him not only to follow the commandments but to sell all he has and give to the poor. Such a command is clearly irrational to the minds of an emergent bourgeoisie. Locke reassures us that this command was "not a standing law of the kingdom; but a probationary command given to this young man to try whether he truly believed him to be the Messiah, and was ready to obey his commands."[9] The note of eschatological urgency, the sudden uncompromising commands to discipleship, are a quandary for Locke, as they were for the theologians in the rationalistic tradition. The eschatological urgency of Jesus' teachings remained a kind of skeleton in the closet until Samuel Reimarus forced modern theology to face the question squarely. Despite his historical concern Locke was not ready for such a confrontation.

Jesus' ethical teachings not only recapitulated the highest ethics of the world's great teachers—Moses, Solon, Confucius—but went beyond them. However, this would have been to no avail if man were to be judged purely on the basis of the "law of works." Legal righteousness demands perfection we cannot attain. "The benefit of life restored by Christ at the resurrection would have been no great advantage, if God had not found out a way to justify some, i.e. so many as obey another law, which God gave . . . called 'the law of faith' "[10] (Rom. 3:27). Although it is impossible to live by the law of works, man can live by the law of faith. "Faith is allowed to supply the defect of full obedience: and so the believers are admitted to life and immortality, as if they were righteous."[11] The justifying faith is belief that Jesus is the Messiah. Locke anticipated his critics, who quickly objected that such a faith is simply the acceptance of a historical fact. The assertion Jesus is the Messiah is not simply a historical statement; it implies action. To believe Jesus is the Messiah means leading a life of repentance and good works. "These two, faith and repentance, i.e. believing Jesus to be the Messiah, and a good life, are the indispensable conditions of the new covenant, to be performed by all those who would obtain eternal life."[12] Faith and repentance are the twofold source of salvation. Human effort is necessary. Man must do the works of repentance. God's graciousness is necessary. God forgives the imperfections men cannot overcome by their best efforts. By his power as Son, Jesus gives to men the immortality he received from his Father. Jesus derived his immortality by being in the image of the Father. The believer receives immortality by being remade in the image of the Son.

This doctrine of salvation neatly touches base on two sharply opposing views. As a loyal son of the Reformation, Locke speaks of "justifying faith" and the impossibility of fulfilling "the law of works." At the same time, he stirs the specter of Pelagianism. He wants to avoid the failure of Lord Herbert, who pictured Jesus as a mere teacher of natural religion. Christ is the Savior without whose help men cannot be freed from the power of sin. Yet no matter how strongly he insists on this, he rejects the idea of total human passivity in salvation. It would violate the most basic moral principle. Each man is responsible for his own sins. Morally it is no more possible to be saved by Christ's merits than to be damned by Adam's sin. The death of Christ does not provide the basis for the law of faith. God's willingness to accept the law of faith instead of the law of works was not created by Christ. It was God's prior graciousness that brought the immortality of Christ to mankind.[13] The death of Christ was not a sacrifice. It was testimony to the truth he proclaimed about God and the ethical life. Jesus is the fearless witness loyal to his message despite persecution and death.

> Another great advantage received by our Savior, is the great encouragement he brought to a virtuous and pious life; great enough to surmount the difficulties and obstacles that lie in the way of it, and reward the pains and hardships of those who stuck firm to their duties, and suffered for the testimony of a good conscience.[14]

Jesus promised the Holy Spirit to his followers to assist them in the moral life. This help comes to us "if we do what we can."

The death of Jesus figures so largely in the New Testament not simply as an example. It is the necessary precondition of the Messiah's greatest miracle, the resurrection. Until the resurrection of Jesus men were uncertain about life after death. There had never been any empirical evidence. The resurrection of Jesus is clear proof of the immortality given to the righteous. Even more important, the resurrection shows Jesus to be the One through whom this immortality comes to men. The Father created a Son who shares his immortality. When by faith and good works men are shaped in the image of the Son they share his immortality.

### *"To Rome by Way of Racovia"*

At no point were the tender nerves of Calvinistic orthodoxy more easily touched than in talk about the cooperation of man in salvation. It is not surprising that Locke was attacked by the Cambridge Calvinist John Edwards. Never wishing to be charged with understating his case, Edwards named his first work *Some Thoughts Concerning the Several Causes and Occasions of Atheism Especially in the Present Age,* and his second, *Socinianism Unmask'd.* Locke made the first and most basic concession to human pride and depravity. He taught that man himself has an essential part in salvation. Then, to deepen the offense, Locke asserted that faith is of no benefit unless joined to repentance revealed by good works. True doctrine is just the opposite for Edwards.

> Our salvation springs from the mere favour and bounty of God through his Son Jesus Christ, and that this is the only source of that happiness which we expect. . . . Where there is not this persuasion and belief, the true notion of Christianity vanishes, and the conceit of merit comes in its room.[15]

In any doctrine allowing "the conceit of merit," Edwards finds two enemies of evangelical Christianity: Socinianism, the error originating in Racovia, and Catholicism, the error stemming from Rome. So he warns that if we follow Locke, "we shall travel to Rome by way of Racovia."[16] The joining of Unitarian liberalism and Catholic reaction may seem strange. To the trained eye of a Calvinist, they both shared one common heresy: they allowed cooperation between God and man in salvation. Such concessions did not worry many of Locke's Anglican contemporaries. For a doctrinaire Calvinist this concession leads inevitably to the works righteousness of Rome or the atheism of the Socinians. The logic of the situation seemed clear enough to Edwards. It is the age-old problem of never letting the nose of the camel in the tent.

Edwards went beyond blanket condemnations into an analysis of Locke's exegesis of Scripture. Locke had taken as his own a theme at the center of Calvinistic theology: the restoration of authentic Christianity by a return to Scriptures. The restoration was to result from historical reading of the New Testament against its Jewish background. This called for valuing some parts of even the New Testament itself more highly than others. The center of Scripture is the Gospels and The Acts, while the epistles have less importance. To commend the Messiahship of Jesus to the Jews, the author of Hebrews used the language of the Hebrew sacrificial system. To commend Jesus to the Gentiles, Paul used the juridical language of ancient Rome. As helpful as this may have been at the time, such teaching cannot be held as truth necessary for salvation. The original, apostolic preachers were unlearned men. They were less tempted to add their own ideas or philosophical speculation to the pure message of Jesus. Because of Paul's greater intellectual sophistication his writings must be approached with care. By assigning less authority to the epistles Locke undercut the Scriptural basis for the doctrines of Calvinism that he found so odious. The epistles show, Edwards contends, "grand heads of Christian divinity, viz. the corruption and degeneracy of human nature, . . . our restoration and reconciliation by Christ's blood, the eminency and excellency of his priesthood, and efficacy of his death, and full satisfaction thereby made the divine justice, and his being made an all sufficient sacrifice for sin."[17] Such heads of divinity Locke found not so grand. Edwards was willing to admit that doctrinal development had taken place between the preaching of Christ and the fuller doctrinal system of the epistles. "The discovery of the doctrines of the Gospel was gradual. . . . We are not to think then that all necessary doctrines of the Christian religion were clearly published in our Saviour's time."[18] But in contrast to Locke, Edwards' contention was that the whole of the Bible is necessary for salvation and is binding on the conscience.

The charge of atheism was leveled against Locke's supposed Socinianism because it was believed all Socinians were but thinly veiled atheists. The logic was clear to the orthodoxy of the day and was fully accepted by Edwards. Socinians deny the Trinity. To deny the Trinity is to take the first and decisive step toward atheism. Edwards was well aware of the implications of the Lockean exegesis of such crucial phrases as "Son of God," "Messiah," and "Word of God." Locke's historical exegesis pointed in the opposite direction from the traditional dogmatic interpretation. In the light of the Old Testament, Messiah and Son of God are equivalent terms. Son of God is not a metaphysical notion. Jesus is called Son of God because he was "conceived in the womb of a virgin by the immediate power of God."[19] He is not an eternally preexistent being along with the Father. The preexistent word of God for Locke was the eternal counsel of the Father to speak his saving word to mankind. To make of the Father's eternal counsel a separate being is an unwarranted speculation. The Son, as the Messiah, is one chosen by God for a special mission and endowed with divine powers to fulfill it. Edwards was not content to let history overthrow dogma in any such fashion. His refutation of Locke did not stem from differing historical evidence. More basic to Edwards was his conviction that Trinitarian orthodoxy provided the only valid framework for exegesis. Locke was betrayed into a misunderstanding of these vital terms, Edwards argued, because of his failure to place them in their proper place in the doctrinal structure.

> The Messias is a title of Christ's office: the Son of God is the title of his divinity. The former is founded on his mission from the Father: the latter on his peculiar property as he is the Second Person of the Trinity; and consequently they are not synonymous terms.[20]

For Edwards, dogma overcomes history.

## The Empiricism of Miracles

If the claim—Jesus is the Messiah—is true, it must be open to empirical verification. The New Testament makes three claims relevant to establishing its truth: Christ was the fulfillment of Old Testament prophecy; he had the power to work miracles; he taught an ethic uniquely sublime and revelatory of the highest good. For Locke, it was the miracles that played the major role in validating the ministry of Christ. In seizing so boldly on the miracles, Locke seems to be making broad concessions to prevailing orthodoxy at the price of alienating his scientific contemporaries. Such was not the case. He gave a centrality to the miracle apologetic far greater than that given in any of the major theological systems of that day. Apologetic theologians had long recognized the ambiguities in any proof from miracles. The basic tendency in the major systems of theology, both Catholic and Protestant, was to count the miracles only one of a number of criteria establishing the authority of Christ. Archbishop Laud reflected this ambiguity: "Miracles, though they were very great inducements of belief, yet were neither evident and convincing proofs, alone and of themselves: both because there may be counterfeit miracles, and because true ones are neither infallible nor inseparable marks of truth in doctrine."[21] As the other "marks of truth in doctrine" on which theology depended lost their convincing power for Locke and his contemporaries, miracles gained a new ascendancy. To turn to miracles was not to repudiate scientific empiricism. Miracles were the data for a new theological empiricism. Locke believed God could make exceptions to the orderliness of his universe when circumstances necessitated. Man's bondage to sin and death was the radical evil that called for such direct divine intervention. Above all else, there was clear evidence of such miraculous intervention in the New Testament.

> The evidence of our Saviour's mission from heaven is so great, in the multitude of miracles he did before all sorts of people, that what he delivered cannot but be received as the oracles of God, and unquestionable verity. For the miracles he did were so ordered by the divine providence and wisdom, that they never were, nor could be denied by any of the enemies, or opposers of Christianity.[22]

The miracles of the New Testament were sound empirical evidence no scientist could ignore. Their certainty had not yet been shaken by critical historians. Such certainty was to last but few years more.

Locke rejected the traditional proofs of revelation through authority of the church, as in Catholicism, or inner testimony of the Holy Spirit to Scripture, as in Protestantism. All claims to church authority turn on a vicious circle of illogic. No one can prove the truth of his statements simply by insisting that all his statements are true because he says them. Nor is the assertion of strong personal conviction believed to come from the Holy Spirit much help. Such subjectivism leads men into intellectual absurdities and moral enormities. The empirical evidence of miracles provides the only convincing proof of revelation. The miracle is not simply an unusual event "contrary to the established course of nature." It is an event for the observer which "is taken by him to be divine."[23] It is only as a miracle testifies to truths "relating to the glory of God, and some great concern of men," that it gains importance as the validation of revelation.[24] The miracle validates the message of its doer by showing that he speaks not by his own power or right but as the agent of some-one greater. Jesus' message is validated by miracles that reveal a power which can come only from God. Yet it is not simply the power of his miracles. They are uniquely appropriate to reveal the message of the Kingdom of God. The miracles show what life in the Kingdom is to be. It is freedom from suffering, want, and death. The miracles of healing, feeding, and resur-rection reveal Jesus as the King whose power to destroy the ancient enemies of mankind will bring the Kingdom of bliss and immortality.

## What Price Clarity?

The comprehensiveness of Locke's Christology made it not so much a formula to be accepted as a program for further in-vestigation. Far more was implicit in the formula "Jesus is the Messiah" than Locke had explicated. For those who shared his starting point but not his reserve, the drive for greater clarity opened two possibilities. One was a Unitarianism like that of Stephen Nye (1648–1719). The other option was the so-called Arianism of the Latitudinarian churchman Samuel Clarke (1675–1729). Nye and Clarke shared with Locke his rejec-tion of deism. They did not believe that natural religion alone was enough. They were both committed to the notion of a revelation in Jesus, verified by miracles. They were at one in rejecting a double standard of truth for science and religion. Reason and experience are the judge in all questions of truth. There cannot be a conflict, as Clarke explained, "else man is unavoidably under the absurdity of being obliged to obey two contrary masters."[25] But on the question of the Trinity, Nye felt the time for judiciously skirting the issue was at an end.

As the trinity has by its natural absurdity and impossibility given a check and stop to the progress of the Gospel so ever since it has served to propagate deism and atheism, and to hinder the conversion of the Jews and Mahometans and the heathen not yet turned to Christianity.[26]

Muhammadans have made great progress in their mission because of "the naturalness of their belief." Efforts to refine the language about the Persons of the Trinity help the matter not one whit. Nye pours his scorn on the "doctrine of three almighty and equal persons, spirits, modes, subsistences, or somewhats in God." The doctrine adds nothing to piety. It has no support in Scripture. Trinitarian speculation is the outcome of the introduction of pagan philosophy by "the platonic philosophers when they came over to Christianity." Nye made a shrewd observation about the anomaly of Trinitarianism in Protestantism. If Protestants reject tradition as the word of man in favor of Scripture as the Word of God, what grounds do they have for holding to a doctrine of the Trinity? Its sole support is human tradition, and only the authority of tradition can keep such a doctrine alive. As Nye bluntly challenged his Protestant contemporaries, "The first-born of the Trinity was the Supremacy of the Pope."[27] Trinitarianism was not the consensus of the early church but a doctrine imposed by a few. Nye was raising a question that Protestantism at the time could neither hear nor answer. How can Trinitarianism be defended on Biblical grounds, when the Bible is read historically? It would take an exegesis far different from the one that dominated orthodoxy.

Hidden in Trinitarianism was another doctrine repellent to sound moral sense—the substitutionary atonement. The notion of the second Person of the Trinity becoming incarnate to provide satisfaction to the first Person is a denial of the gracious freedom of God. Jesus was sent by the Father to declare forgiveness to all who turn from their wicked ways and enter the Kingdom. Trinitarianism is also in danger of Docetism. No matter how stated, Nye argues, the Athanasian doctrine of the Christ's divinity denies his humanity. Jesus is a true human being, although he is the Son of God by virtue of his virgin birth and his baptism. The unique character of Jesus is best revealed in what he does rather than in speculations about his being.

> Christ is God with respect to the empire which he hath received from God over the new creatures which he hath taken out of the chaos of sin, and governs by his Father's power: But with respect to God his Father, he is only the minister

of his will, his messenger, and is at most called Lord . . . to denote him whom the Father hath made his Lieutenant, who hath received his empire from another and is to deliver it to him that entrusted him with it.[28]

Nye has the distinction of having coined a unique Christological title—Lieutenant. But his ingenuity fails him when it comes to delineating exactly what God's Lieutenant revealed over and beyond natural religion.

In his major exegetical work, *The Scripture Doctrine of the Trinity,* Clarke argues for a doctrine of Christ that stands between Unitarianism and orthodoxy. Like Nye or Locke, Clarke sees church history as the obscuring of the light of truth once so clear in Jesus and the apostles. Being a better historian than either Nye or Locke, Clarke understood the development of doctrine more accurately. Even though the Scriptures contain "the whole and only rule of truth in matters of religion," they are difficult to understand in places. Hence, the church developed "an extract of the rule of truth" in the form of baptismal creeds which contained "the fundamental articles of faith."

> But in the process of time, as men grew less pious, and more contentious; so in the several churches they enlarged their creeds and confessions of faith; and grew more minute in determining unnecessary controversies.[29]

Human speculations grew apace "from small beginnings to greater and greater certainty. But matters of revelation and divine testimony are, on the contrary, complete at first; and the Christian religion was most perfect at the beginning." Matters decayed "till at last revelation was swallowed up in the great apostasy. Out of which it began to recover in good measure at the reformation."[30] The reform of doctrine by Scripture can never be done so long as men start with their ideas and move to Scripture to find proof texts. Instead, they must start with Scripture and read it in terms of itself.

Clarke rejects the Unitarian interpretation of John 1:1. The preexistent Logos is not the interior reason of the Father that inspires the man Jesus. The plain sense of Scripture gives the lie to such assertions. Instead, the Logos is a person who created the world. He is a person called "God by communication of divinity from him who is of himself God."[31] When Jesus says, "The Father is greater than I," he undermines any notion that the Son has the same self-existent being as the Father. The Father alone is "the one Supreme Cause and Original of Things; one, simple, uncompounded, intelligent Agent or Person. . . . The Son is not Self-existent; but derives his being and all his attributes from the Father as from the Supreme Cause."[32] The Son is sometimes called God in the New Testament. This is an account of his divine authority over us. "The Scriptures never professedly mention any metaphysical notions, only moral doctrines."[33] The Bible speaks of "personal characters, offices, powers and attributes" rather than "supposedly metaphysical nature." "But how his being was derived; or what the figurative word 'begotten' properly and literally implies, this the Scripture hath no where revealed or explained."[34] The label of Arianism was quickly attached to Clarke's Christology by his opponents. Clarke rejects the term himself, for, he argues, the Arians, like their orthodox opponents, were wrongly certain about something really unknowable. They believed they knew exactly how the Father and the Son are related. Clarke contends that we simply do not know.

The essentially subordinationist Christology that Clarke championed had been scouted earlier in the seventeenth century by poets and philosophers. Newton's Christology was of this sort, as was that of John Milton. While it was convenient to brand these as Arian for polemic purposes, Clarke was right in repudiating the term. The aim was not to espouse heresy against orthodoxy but to get behind the metaphysical tangles of the fourth century. In his *Treatise on Christian Doctrine,* Milton reveals great care in defining Christological terminology in the light of early levels of tradition, instead of in conformity with Nicene orthodoxy. By historical analysis he had peeled away one layer of tradition to find an earlier one. The Athanasian orthodoxy was rejected for the subordinationist Christology of the earlier fathers which was defined in Biblical, not philosophical, terms.[35] Clarke's aim was to make a definition of orthodoxy based on the personalistic, moral categories of the New Testament instead of metaphysically defined ones.

The issue of the subordination of Christ to the Father was an apt starting point for such a program of reformulation. Orthodox theology was in a paradoxical situation on this question. On the one hand, there were those New Testament passages which picture the Son as subordinate to the Father. On the other hand, there was the necessity of maintaining the unchangingly divine nature of the Son, as dictated by the use of the term "homoousios." This paradox had been resolved by the introduction of the doctrine of the dual states of Christ. During his earthly ministry, he was in the state of exinanition, or humiliation, in which "Christ as it were divested himself of divinity, the same being hidden and has appeared in the form of a servant." In this state, he can be said to be inferior to the Father. In resurrection and ascension, he returns to the state of exaltation in which his fully divine nature is revealed. As the Calvinist Henrici à Diest explained it, "The state of exaltation is that in which, redemption accomplished, Christ was borne to the height of glory, the human nature being glorified, whereas the divine glory was manifested a second time."[36] Christ was always homoousios with the Father. What varied was whether the divinity was hidden or manifest. Clarke asked the critical question: Why posit an underlying equality between Father and Son, when there is no direct evidence for it? Clarke, like Locke, looks to Newton's prohibition against positing "occult qualities" for which there are no data. The Biblical evidence points to subordination followed by exaltation. It is not necessary to posit an unchanging equality with the Father to prove that Christ is the Savior. God has clearly designated him for this task by his unique birth, his miracles, and his resurrection. The divinity of Christ is grounded in his God-given mission, not in some unprovable notion of his being. Clarke was not trying to resuscitate an ancient heresy but to develop a new method of theologizing, the method of empiricism. His orthodox contemporaries were unable to see the Nicene definition of orthodoxy as a development from Scripture. They believed it to be simply a restatement of Scripture. As a result Clarke and his followers labored under the charge of Arianism. Yet the charge was irrelevant. They sought not an old heresy but a new way of thinking in theology.

*Chapter V*

# DEISM,

# DOUBT, AND HISTORY

*No Orthodoxy but the Truth*

The noise and the heat of controversy stirred by Locke were but a small beginning of the whirlwind loosed by John Toland (1670–1722) in his *Christianity Not Mysterious* which appeared a year after *The Reasonableness of Christianity*. Toland, a young Irishman, had left the Catholicism of his parents and "the idolatry of papist religion." He had launched himself on a collision course with the religious establishments in his search for a religion free of superstition, idolatry, and finally even mystery. His commitment was to no orthodoxy defined by church or council. He feated no indictment of heresy. "The Imputation of *Heterodoxy* being now liberal upon the slightest Occasions, out of Ignorance, Passion, or Malice . . . , it is many times instead of a Reproach the greatest Honour imaginable." His commitment was to "no ORTHODOXY but the TRUTH."[1] His orthodoxy was the truth of rationally proved, clearly stated doctrines. Within two years of its publication, *Christianity Not Mysterious* had been answered by thirty-five books, countless sermons, pastoral letters, and legal condemnations. The hangman burned it in Dublin by order of the Irish Parliament. Toland was excluded from all chances for ecclesiastical or academic preferments. His situation was not helped by what his friend William Molyneux called "his exceeding great value of himself."

Although later in life Toland claimed he had tried to suppress *Christianity Not Mysterious* as a "youthful indiscretion," it had irretrievably become a link in unfolding the new theology.

Toland's work is not strikingly original. He takes his lead, as did Locke, from the unfolding of the New Testament confession "Jesus is the Messiah." He utilizes the argument from miracles and fulfilled prophecy. The crucial shift is in testing the rationality of the doctrines of Scripture. Toland tightened the rationalistic criticism. For Locke, revelation could not be irrational, yet it could be above reason. Toland took the next step: "There is nothing in the Gospel contrary to reason or above it." Such shadings of meaning could well have been overlooked save for the polemic and popular style of Toland's writing. He wrote not a monograph to be pondered by intellectuals but a tract addressed to every man, calling him to use his God-given reason in religion. Here was a challenge that could not be ignored or endured by the orthodox.

Since John Leland put Toland and the other deists into perspective in *A View of the Principal Deistical Writers* (1754), a pattern was set for the interpretation of deism. English deism and its continuation in the French Enlightenment has been viewed as a movement of rationalistic religious criticism aimed against Christianity. Such an interpretation obscures as much as it reveals about the meaning and aims of the English deists. It is true that the historical Biblical criticism utilized by the French came from the English deists. Voltaire, the Encyclopedists, and even Rousseau, raided the writings not only of the deists but even of churchmen like Clarke for evidence against Christianity. But this does not prove that their intentions were identical, although Leland implies this. "Deism" had been in use since the sixteenth century to describe belief in the sufficiency of natural religion without revelation. In popular use it was not so much the description of a theology as its condemnation. Toland, the supposed initiator of popular deism, repudiates the term. His professed aim is not to cause unbelief, but to remove it. "But it is visible to everyone that they are the *Contradictions* and *Mysteries* unjustly charged upon *Religion,* which occasion so many to become *Deists* and *Atheists*."[2] He as willingly joined deism with atheism as the orthodox and gladly poked fun at the Socinians and Arians for worshiping "a creature God." His intention was not to destroy Christianity but to return it to its original purity by rational, historical criticism. English deism springs more from the typically Protestant drive for reform by repristination than from an anti-Christian movement for destruction by criticism. Its failure to achieve this goal should not obscure its intention. English deism revealed in its growth and culmination the unsolved problem of the new Protestantism, the problem of authority. How is it possible to relate the prophetic principle of rational, historical criticism to the substantive affirmations of Christian faith? Would not the criticism of superstition and idolatry erode the uniqueness of the Christian faith when applied repeatedly? Is it possible to separate by reason the "overbelief" of the superstitious from essential Christianity? Deism answered yes. History proved it wrong. Not only the perversions but also the center of Biblical faith collapsed under the probing of criticism. The failure of the deists to solve this problem stemmed from their assumption of a simple, direct continuity between revelation and reason. Having been critical of many things, they failed to be critical of reason itself.

Rationality in religion for Toland comes in the rejection of the mysterious because the basic character of knowledge is clarity. "If Things be deliver'd in Words not understood by the Hearer, nor demonstrated to agree with other Truths already very clear, or now so made to him, he cannot conceive 'em."[3] If a religious doctrine is said to be mysterious in the sense of being intellectually unclear, it has thereby no high claim to authority. Such doctrines are simply gibberish, like the ecstatic speech of a man speaking in tongues. Toland rejects the conclusion many were ready to draw that the denial of mystery is the denial of revelation. Revelation is a means of gaining information. Although man has the capacity to judge the rationality of a supposed revelation, he does not have the capacity to create or invent the revealed ideas. It was precisely his empiricism that ensured the idea of revelation for Toland. Reason is the capacity to judge the data that man receives. It is not, as in the rationalistic natural theology of Lord Herbert, the power to spin a doctrine of God out of the mind alone. Revelation is not the grounds for proving the truth of an idea. Unlike the orthodox, he declares, "I said REVELATION was not a necessitating Motive of Assent, but a *Means of Information.*"[4]

Toland's confidence in the ability of reason to discern truth in the information that comes to it allowed a fresh perspective on miracles. Confidence in man's rationality allowed the question of authority, miracle, and prophecy to be brought under a fuller historical scrutiny than Locke allowed. The appeal of the argument from fulfilled prophecy was mainly to Jesus' Jewish contemporaries. But even to them the convincing force of fulfilled prophecy was limited. It was rather the miracles, and more specifically the miraculous works Scripture prophesied that the Messiah would do, that persuaded men. The convincing power of the miracles will be evident to any men who "read the sacred Writings with that Equity and Attention that is due to meer Humane Works: Nor is there any different Rule to be followed in the Interpretation of Scripture from what is common to all other Books."[5] The New Testament must be read not only in the light of the Old Testament but also specifically in the light of the Talmud. Toland was one of the first to identify the importance of the setting of primitive Christianity in Rabbinic Judaism, although he does not relinquish a disparaging estimate of it. "We have the *Talmud,* and other Works of the Rabbins, which however otherwise useless, give us no small Light into the Ancient Rites and Language."[6] Yet even when Scripture is read in its historic setting, the critical task is not finished. Miracles are not only acts "which the Laws of NATURE cannot perform by their ordinary Operations," but they must not be contrary to reason. "Now whatever is contrary to *Reason* can be no *Miracle.* . . . *Contradiction* is only another word for Impossible or Nothing. The *miraculous* Action therefore must be something in itself intelligible and possible, though the manner of doing it be extraordinary."[7] This allows setting aside all the non-Christian miracles plus those of the papist. The irrationality of spurious miracles is not so much a question of the irrationality of the event as of the teaching it supports. Even though Toland did not deny the Scriptural miracles, he did open the question of evaluating them by the rules of historical evidence. He holds miracles valid only if done in public and, specifically, in the presence of an unbeliever. The question was just how long the Scriptural witness to miracles could hold up under the repeated application of such scrutiny?

Toland's conviction that Jesus was the teacher of a rational, universal religion, instead of the irrational counterfeit which had replaced it in churchly Christianity, led him to search for further documentary proof than that found in the New Testament. He believed he had found such evidence in a text called *Nazarenus,* to which he gives the subtitle *Jewish, Gentile and Mahometan Christianity.*[8] Toland believed that the Jewish Christians preserved a purer version of Jesus' teachings than had the Gentiles. He believed he had a document linking the Jewish Christians or Nazarenes, as he called them, to the Muhammadans. The document sets forth a universal moral religion taught by Jesus. Actually, Toland was dealing with a fifteenth-century Italian forgery written by an unknown convert from Christianity to Islam. His convictions about the rationality of primitive Christianity carried him far beyond the evidence, as Lorenz von Mosheim, the great German church historian, was to show within a few years of the publication of *Nazarenus.* Toland's forays into the field of church history point to a crucial connection in the new Christologies between rationalistic and historical criticism. The religion of Jesus was assumed to be rational. Historical criticism was to strip away perversions obscuring this basic truth.

## Examining the Evidences

Toland's invitation to "read the sacred Writings with that Equity and Attention that is due meer Humane Works" was abundantly heeded by his deist contemporaries. Anthony Collins (1676–1729) in his *Discourse of the Grounds and Reasons of the Christian Religion* (1724) and *The Scheme of Literal Prophecy Considered* (1727) was to subject the evidences of fulfilled prophecy to decisive criticism. Collins in his *Discourse of Freethinking* (1713) had issued a manifesto and slogan for an age which wanted to free itself of every authority save that of reason alone. Now he was to apply the rule of free thought to a matter of great moment in the life of the church. Unlike Toland, Collins was an English gentleman independently wealthy and free to follow his research. Like his fellow theological rationalists of the time, Collins was convinced it was the self-interest of the clerical hierarchy that blocked the application of reason to religious matters. The storm of protest that his work engendered provided him ample justification for his belief about the clergy. Thomas Woolston (1670–1733) joined in the critical work of Collins, investigating the proofs of the divinity of Christ's mission. In his series of six *Discourses on the Miracles of Our Saviour* (1727–1730), Woolston probed into Locke's vital assumption that the New Testament gives accurate reports of the miracles. Woolston sought to find whether the miracle stories "contained all the true characters of historical evidences." When he concluded negatively on this matter he felt the full brunt of official censorship. Unprotected by influential friends or independent means, he lost his Cambridge fellowship, was fined and put in prison, where he died in 1733, a martyr to freedom of thought in theology.

Collins and Woolston were interested in the argument from fulfilled prophecy because of the weakness of the miracle apologetic. They accepted the miraculous in the life of Jesus. But there is a wide gap between affirming miracles in general and proving a miracle in particular. Woolston perceived the impossibility of concluding from Jesus' miracles the belief that he should be "guide of our conscience, ruler of our hearts and the author of a religion."[9] Miracles do not necessarily support the specifically Christian assertions about God and morality. Collins argued that "miracles were to move and dispose men to receiving the truth."[10] They do not themselves contain the truth. Yet even more basic was the fear of false miracles. Toland and Locke disposed of the miracles of heathens and papists. Woolston took the next step by asking whether the New Testament contains false reports of miracles. Difficulties abound in the New Testament reports. They do not have proper evidence. The transfiguration was done in a cloud; hence there were no impartial witnesses to know what really happened. The healings would require examination by a competent physician to ensure their validity. While personally confessing faith in Jesus' resurrection, Woolston said the Gospel records are confused and contradictory. Woolston's questions about the resurrection were answered by Thomas Sherlock in *The Trail of the Witnesses of the Resurrection of Jesus,* one of the most popular antideistic writings of the time. But Sherlock was so much of a rationalist himself that his answers proved anything but final. Once launched on the road of rational, historical study nothing could stand unchallenged. The challenge was accepted by Peter Annet (1693–1769), who undertook a thoroughgoing historical analysis of the Easter story. For Annet the inner contradictions point to the basically nonhistorical character of the resurrection. The doubts Woolston raised as a question had with Annet become the final answer.

In his analysis of the New Testament miracle stories Woolston does not seek to preserve their historicity by rationalistic reinterpretations. Woolston sees miracle stories as an expression of the myth-making tendencies at work in early Christianity. Miracle stories are symbolic accounts of how Jesus works to save men. Jesus' mission was in curing "those distempers of the soul, that metaphorically pass under the name of blindness, lameness, deafness, etc. . . . For the proof of his divine authority and messiahship, which is only to be proved by his mysterious works, of which those done in the flesh are but type and figure."[11] Woolston does not accept allegory simply to elude the problematic character of miracles. Instead, he argues, he is reading miracle stories as did the fathers of the early church. Literalism cannot claim antiquity. Early Christians were willing to accept the allegorical and symbolic as part of Scripture.

Collins realized that the fast-developing miracle critique placed the question of the fulfillment of prophecy in a new and crucial light. Fulfilled prophecy was the central means of validating Jesus' Messiahship. The apostle Paul, Collins maintained, believed that Jesus was the Messiah not simply because he was raised on the third day but because he was "raised on the third day according to the Scriptures." Collins could even quote Jesus himself in support of the superiority of fulfilled prophecy as a validation of his mission. "If they heed not Moses and the prophets, what profit is there if one should rise from the dead." Prophecies are "perpetual and standing miracles and do not disappear, like other miracles on their performance."[12] They are specific in meaning, whereas a miracle is not. The specific works of the Messiah as Moral Teacher, Head of the Kingdom of God, as well as occurrences in his life, as his virgin birth, death, and resurrection, are foretold. But no matter how exact, the fulfillments are based upon "a secondary, or typical, or allegorical, or enigmatical sense, that is, in a sense different from the obvious and literal sense, which they bear in the Old Testament."[13] The literal sense of the prophecies relates to events during the time of the prophets themselves. As Collins compared the prophecy of the virgin birth in Isa. 7:14 to its fulfillment in Matt. 1:22, he separated the literal from the figurative fulfillment. When Isaiah spoke of a young woman living in the days of Ahaz giving birth to a child, he referred to the coming of a son of the prophet. The birth of the child was to be a sign to Ahaz of the validity of the prophet's message. It would make no sense if the birth did not occur until centuries later. In its original historical setting the prophecy was literally fulfilled during the lifetime of the prophet. It was fulfilled a second time in the birth of Jesus. This fulfillment is seen only in the light of an allegorical interpretation of the prophecy.

The response of deism's opponents to Collins' analysis of prophecy was that nonliteral fulfillment is really no fulfillment at all. Protestant theology had become increasingly devoted to literalism during the period of orthodoxy. Not only the rigid doctrine of inspiration but also the Protestant polemic against the allegorical exegesis of Roman Catholicism had focused attention upon the literal meaning of the Bible. At this point, Collins and Woolston made a sound historical observation. Allegorical exegesis and argumentation were accepted procedures for theology in the ancient world. The Jewish rabbis and the early church fathers were not bound to the literal sense of Scripture. To interpret the New Testament in its own terms is to accept allegory and symbol. Allegorical exegesis as practiced in the ancient world was not arbitrary. It had its own rules of procedure. Collins turned for evidence to the earlier work of Hugo Grotius and the great Dutch Hebraist Wilhelm Surenhusius (d. 1698), who had analyzed the rules of allegorical exegesis. The rules governing allegorical interpretation and reasoning were different from those of scholastic or even commonsense reasoning. To read the Bible in terms of itself was to journey into a land foreign to one's own.

As important as the work of Collins, Woolston, and Annet was for the growth of historical understanding, these men had not resolved the apologetic question of modern theology. They had cast it in a new and more difficult light. Locke had pictured Christianity as the perfect expression of natural religion supported by the irrefutable evidence of miracles and fulfilled prophecy. Deism not only weakened the historical proofs of Christianity; it had uncovered the mythological side to Christian doctrine in the New Testament. It was no longer possible to maintain that the mythological aspects were a perversion brought by half-converted philosophers or self-seeking priests. Christianity is only the bearer of natural religion when its outer garments of mythology are penetrated by rational analysis. The Socinians could appeal to the New Testament as a whole against the perversions of churchly teaching. Locke could point to the Gospels and primitive preaching against church doctrine. Now was there any point in history that a valid account of religious truth could be found, save as men grasp it by reason alone?

## *The Unchanging Gospel*

In Matthew Tindal (1656–1733) the inner logic of the deist Christology reached its inevitable conclusion. He stated the case for a rational Christianity—or "Christian Deism," as he called it—in *Christianity as Old as the Creation, or the Gospel a Republication of the Religion of Nature* (1730). The title of the book was its message in summary. Tindal went beyond Toland, who still believed in revelation to supply men with information they would not otherwise have. For Tindal human rationality meant not only the power to judge the true and false in religion but also to know what is necessary to please God. The argument stemmed from his understanding of the justice of God. Tindal argued from the just and unchanging being of God to the unchanging nature of his demands on man. Special revelations, imposing special obligations, are unthinkable. God plays no favorites. No man is excluded from salvation for not having lived in the time and place where the supposedly saving revelation is made known. There is only one saving truth and that is "as old as Creation." The truth of Christianity lies in its conformity with this unchanging religion of nature. To make good his claim, Tindal expanded the scope of reason. Locke held an aristocratic view of reason, arguing that while in principle reason can be the sufficient guide to truth, in fact it was not for most men. Tindal democratized reason. "It is common to the unlearned as well as learned; for have not all alike faculties given by God, to distinguish between good and evil; right and wrong."[14] If reason were not universally found in men, they could not be held responsible for their violations of the law. Tindal defended this view of reason as a continuation of that taken by churchmen, even the antideistic Bishop Sherlock. Tindal maintained that he was simply extending the high appraisal of reason already part of Christianity.

> True religion, and that which is from God, was, and is, and ever will be the same in substance in all countries . . . ; and the sum of it is, *To love the Lord our God with all our hearts, and with all our minds, and with all our strength; and* next to that, *to love our neighbors as ourselves.* This was the religion that the patriarchs, and all the pious men of old lived in; when as yet there was no revealed instituted religion in the world. —That this is the sum of Christian religion, no man can in the least doubt, that has ever read the new testament.[15]

All the traditional doctrines of the person and work of Christ are eliminated save one. Christ is to call men to repentance. "The end of Christ's coming seems not to teach men new duties, but to repent of the breach of known duties. And when it was objected to him, that he kept company with sinners, he owns the charge, and says, the whole need no physician, but they that are sick; which would have been an improper answer, if he thought that all stood in need of him, and his spiritual physic."[16] Some men were already acceptable to God by their obedience to his will. It was only those who were heedless in their sins that had to be made aware of their failure. The teachings of Jesus are revelation only in the light of the very special use Tindal makes of that term. Revelation cannot be the disclosure of something not already knowable. It is the direct imparting of truth by one person to another. This personal communication of the truths of religion by Jesus became the basis for Christianity as an institutional religion. Such personal communication Jesus used in calling men to repentance. No matter how important personal communication may be in calling men to repentance, it is not to be exempted from rational scrutiny.

Tindal's doctrine of reconciliation has nothing to do with the forgiveness of sins. The reconciliation of God and man comes through living by the rules of right reason. Tindal translates the deification theory of atonement, like that in Irenaeus and Athanasius, into rationalistic terms. The root of the doctrine is in the nature of God. God is "a Being absolutely perfect, and infinitely happy in himself, who is the source of all other beings; and that what perfections soever the creatures have, they are wholly derived from him."[17] The happiness of God consists in the exact agreement of every aspect of the divine being. There is in God no tension between will and nature, between thinking and doing, as there is in man. This perfection of God can be given to man to the extent to which he lives in accord with right reason. "We then, . . . *live the life of God;* and there would be no difference between his life and ours; . . . we should be made partakers of the divine nature, be born of God, and be perfect as our heavenly father is perfect; and can that be without being as happy as we are perfect?" The key to deification is man's rational nature. "It is our reason which makes us the image of God himself, and is the common bond which unites Heaven and Earth; the creatures and creator."[18] For Tindal, reason is more than the good servant of utilitarianism; it is man's link with God and eternal blessedness. He opens the possibility of translating the language of Christology into a doctrine of man. But Tindal did not more than glimpse this possibility. The conversion of Christology into anthropology was to await an outburst of romantic imagination in another century beyond the ken of Tindal and his contemporaries.

## Miracles Past and Present

Deism had questioned the evidence for miracles. David Hume (1711–1776) drew the vital conclusion that rendered the miracle apologetic no longer viable. He turned the question of miracle and revelation to a new direction. Hume may well seem a strange person to include in a history of Christology. He gave little specific attention to Jesus. Yet he was crucial in creating the intellectual atmosphere in which Christology was formulated. *An Enquiry Concerning Human Understanding* contains his analysis of miracle and fulfilled prophecy. His attack on the ·adequacy of the miracle apologetic was not new, nor was it in theory as crucial to the future of theology as his later analysis of natural religion. But his arguments on miracles were simpler and more direct in their effect than his later work. The reaction of churchmen to Hume reflects the basic changes theology had undergone in the eighteenth century. Orthodoxy was being stated and defended in terms set by Locke and the deists. Orthodox apologists, like Bishop Butler in his *The Analogy of Religion,* stated the case for Christianity in terms of natural religion and the miracle apologetic. Miracles provided the basis for moving from the foundation of natural religion to the distinctive doctrines of Christianity. The reserve of earlier theologians about the usefulness of the miracle apologetic was gone. Conservatives as well as the innovators in theology accepted the same definition of the problem. The critical difference was the inability of the conservatives to move from their increasingly untenable position on the historicity of miracles. Deism, secure in its belief in the sufficiency of natural religion, could scrutinize the miracles freely. Orthodoxy was committed to the more perilous path of having to validate the distinctive part of its message by the historicity of Christ's miracles. Hume's public and polemic refutation of this possibility became the wedge being driven between the church and the new Christology.

Hume proposes his argument about miracles as a protection against bigotry, superstition, and delusion in religion. He examines reasoning "derived from the testimony of men, and the reports of eye-witnesses and spectators."[19] How can we evaluate the evidence for past events? In part, we determine the believability of a report by the conformity of what is reported to our normal expectations for such things happening. We judge in the light of what past experience has taught. In part, we judge reports of past events by our confidence in the trustworthiness of the reporter. Most men have "an inclination to truth and a principle of probity." So we may safely accept their reports as accurate. At times this is not the case. "A man delirious, or noted for falsehood and villainy, had no manner of authority with us."[20] Following these two rules—conformity with the observed course of nature and determination of the reliability of witnesses—the accuracy of information can be measured. Assurance varies "from the highest certainty to the lowest species of moral evidence." "A wise man," Hume argues, "proportions his belief to the evidence."[21] Rash conclusions drawn from scanty evidence have no place in the judgment of the wise man. It is very possible for the historian or philosopher to weigh evidence with cool sagacity and live happily with tentative conclusions. But can such be the case with the believer in a religion claiming finality? The analysis of the possibility of historical knowledge poses insuperable problems for a religion that is validated by miracles. The problem stems from the very nature of miracles themselves. "A miracle is a violation of the laws of nature; and as a firm and unalterable experience has established these laws, the proof against a miracle, from the very nature of the fact, is as entire as any argument from experience can possibly make it."[22] The report of a miracle fails the first test of evidence. It is not in conformity with the observed course of nature. Hume is not arguing like Spinoza in a metaphysical fashion against the possibility of a miracle. He remains true to his empiricism. Miracles are at least a theoretical possibility. His real concern is the evidence needed to establish the occurrence of a miracle. His conclusion is that such evidence is never available.

> No testimony is sufficient to establish a miracle, unless the testimony be of such a kind, that its falsehood would be more miraculous, than the fact, which it endeavours to establish; and even in that case there is a mutual destruction of arguments, and the superior only gives us an assurance suitable to that degree of force, which remains, after deducting the inferior.[23]

Miracle stories fail the second test of historical evidence—the reliability of witnesses. "There is not to be found, in all history, any miracle attested by a sufficient number of men, of such unquestioned good-sense, education, and learning, as to secure us against all delusions in themselves. . . . But if the spirit of religion joins itself to the love of wonder, there is an end of common sense."[24] Observers of miracles abound in "ignorant and barbarous nations" and in ancient times. The progression of modern civilization has slowly but certainly eroded the miraculous. The miracle requires for its confirmation a type of testimony that is nowhere available, from a type of witness that does not exist.

Hume ends his chapter on miracles with an enigmatic and much-debated conclusion. Neither miracle nor prophecy can "be proved, so as to be the foundation of a system of religion."[25] The force of this conclusion he states is "to confound those dangerous friends or disguised enemies to the *Christian Religion,* who have undertaken to defend it by the principles of human reason. Our most holy religion is founded on *Faith,* not on reason; and it is a sure method of exposing it to put it to such a trial as it is, by no means, fitted to endure."[26] The rationalizers are the most dangerous foes of true Christianity. The believer who leans on faith and faith alone is on far firmer ground. Then in what seems an about-face Hume finishes: "We may conclude that the *Christian Religion* not only was at first attended with miracles, but even at this day cannot be believed by any reasonable person without one. . . . Whoever is moved by *Faith* to assent to it, is conscious of a continued miracle in his own person, which subverts all the principles of his understanding, and gives him a determination to believe what is most contrary to custom and experience."[27] After a crushing attack on Christianity, Hume seemingly concludes for a highly conservative, even anti-intellectual, version of the faith. His *Dialogues Concerning Natural Religion* concludes with an equally startling turn of argument. He lauds faith as the only possible grounds of Christianity. Hume was arguing in a fashion not unlike another eighteenth-century critic of traditional Christianity, Gotthold Lessing, who could come at times to highly conservative conclusions. Their aim was to expose the underlying and irreducible irrationality of Christianity. Hume swept aside as bad philosophy and shoddy history the attempted modernizations of Christianity. The liberalizers undermined Christianity by trying to temper it with rationalistic apologetics. Christianity is a viable religion only in the light of faith in miracle. Reflecting his Calvinistic upbringing, Hume centers on the miracle of the witness of the Holy Spirit in convincing the believer. Such a miracle of conversion is the only possible grounds on which Christian faith can be rendered believable. But it was precisely this sort of arbitrary subjectivism that was so offensive to the spirit of the Enlightenment. If Christianity can be accepted only on such terms, it is clearly unacceptable. Faith gives men "a determination to believe what is most contrary to custom and experience." Yet "custom and experience" are the guideposts that Hume set as the only protection against superstition and delusion. By his extreme statement of the case Hume brings Christianity as a whole under condemnation.

With the sounding of the Humean trumpet of skepticism the Christologies based on the miracle apologetic did not collapse in a moment. English theology remained wed to them for many years to come. Bishop Butler's *Analogy* was to remain a textbook in theology for English churchmen until replaced by Tractarian and Evangelical doctrine. Hume's arguments were not so much refuted as pushed aside. The continuation of Locke's Christology was in the Unitarianism of late eighteenth-century England and America. Despite the critical work of the deists and Hume, the Lockean Christology was given fresh currency by

Theophilus Lindsey (1723–1808), David Hartley (1705–1757), and Joseph Priestley (1733–1804). With the founding by Lindsey in 1774 of the first Unitarian church in England, Unitarianism forsook its role as a critical movement in the Church of England and among the dissenters to become a separate denomination. As important as this was for the institutional life of this group, from the standpoint of the history of doctrine it is a paradox. Basically, their Christology was the reassertion of Unitarian recension of Locke. The exegetical arguments and the patristic quotations used in the Unitarian tracts and books to defend their position against orthodoxy were those of Nye and Biddle and before them of Crell, Socinus, and even Servetus. Much of this material had been gathered together by Nathaniel Lardner (1684–1768) in his massive work *The Credibility of the Gospel History* which was a source book of patristic and Biblical arguments for religious liberals of the eighteenth century.

While the leaders of Unitarianism in the late eighteenth century were giving this Christology its most eloquent and public expression, they worked out of a tradition that antedated them by a century and that had been under devastating attack by radical deism and by Hume. Thomas Belsham (1750–1829) expressed his bafflement after reading for the first time the seventeenth-century Unitarian tracts, especially those of Nye. "It is very remarkable that Unitarianism, after having made so conspicuous a figure in the latter part of the seventeenth century, should have become totally silent, for the first half of the eighteenth century."[28] This silence was not simply the function of the unpopularity of Unitarianism. At the beginning of the eighteenth century the theological innovators were still eager to think of themselves as churchmen. The Established Church at that time still tolerated liberal clergymen, if only grudgingly. Also, the so-called "Arianism" of Clarke provided a halfway house for those influenced by the new critical Biblicism and scientific empiricism yet not ready for Unitarianism. Arianism allowed them to accept the terms of doctrinal subscription needed for ordination. After the deists and Hume, it became increasingly clear to churchmen that the new theology was a force with which they could not compromise. At the same time, the halfway house of Arianism proved untenable to the liberals after its criticism by Lardner and others. It was Lardner's *Letter Concerning the Logos,* for example, which converted Priestley from Arianism to Unitarianism. The way of either intellectual or institutional compromise was closed. At this point Unitarianism emerged as a denomination. The critical Biblicism and scientific empiricism at work in the Christology of Lindsey, Hartley, and Priestley seemed innovative to their orthodox antagonists. But what they had really done was to bring into clear public view a Christology that had been developing slowly amid the theological underground of early liberalism. One of the ironies of the times was that despite the horrors of the orthodox at the appearance of Unitarianism, there were afoot already new critical movements that undermined the natural religion and miracle apologetics of classical Unitarianism. To see these in their true measure, it is necessary to shift from England to the new center of theological innovation in Germany.

## Chapter VI

# PIETY,

# PHILOSOPHY, AND CHRIST

*England and the Continent*

The acceptance of the new science and philosophy in the theological centers of the Continent lagged far behind England. Scholastic orthodoxy reigned in the theological faculties of Germany. Pietists like Spener and Francke could decry the bareness of a religion based on doctrinal orthodoxy but unconverted lives. Mystics like Tersteegen could shun doctrinal polemics to seek union with the inner life of God. But if a student wanted to take theology seriously at a German university at the beginning of the eighteenth century, he would study the great doctrinal systems of Lutheran or Reformed orthodoxy. Similarly in France, quietistic piety and even Jansenist insubordination had ruffled the life of the church, yet theological faculties still taught and elaborated the growing structure of post-Tridentine Catholicism. Refutations had been made repeatedly by orthodox theologians of the errors of Socinianism, Arminianism, and the egregious infidelity of English deistical writers. Although refuted, these new doctrines did not disappear. The relation of English and German theology in the eighteenth century was just the reverse of what it was to become by the late nineteenth century. The modernizing, liberalizing tendencies flowed from England to the Continent. Locke's *Reasonableness of Chris-*

*tianity* appeared in German translation in 1733. Clarke's *Scripture-Doctrine of the Trinity* was translated by a Halle professor in 1774, while the more radical deistic writers were known by a myriad of tracts rendered into French and German throughout the century.

Reaction to the English religious thought was complex. In France modern thought and Christian theology came to an impasse in which either modernity was viewed as a rejection of faith or faith became the enemy of modernity. As is often the case in such collisions, it brought out the worst in both parties. The shrill arrogance of churchmen was rivaled only by that of the philosophers. Voltaire (François Marie Arouet, 1694–1778) introduced Newtonian physics and English philosophy to France in 1734 with his *Philosophical Letters* and in 1738 with *Elements of the Philosophy of Newton*. Both Voltaire and the French anticlerical writers drew heavily on the arguments supplied by the English deists. In France the faith of the English deists had disappeared. Voltaire saw Jesus as an ethical teacher of rational moral values in the tradition of Confucius and Socrates. He was keenly aware of the difficulties of finding a true picture of Jesus in the Gospels because the records had been so deeply colored by a later Christian faith. However, even after the application of proper critical techniques, the records reveal Jesus as a teacher who strayed from a rational ethic into the superstitions of his time. Voltaire theorized that Jesus compromised with the superstitions of the common people in an effort to raise their moral standards just a little. The resurrection histories arose out of the hatred of the earliest believers against the murderers of Jesus. This invention was taken over by the fanatic Paul and made into the decisive belief for the Christian religion. All else follows from this in dolorous inevitability. The intellectual and political tyranny of Christianity grew step by step as the message of Jesus became submerged under the flood of Platonic philosophy and finally under the power of the state at the time of Constantine.

What is found in Voltaire, or in the even more militant views of J. M. de Maistre and d'Holbach, or in the more sympathetic picture given by Rousseau, is not new historical research. However, critical Biblical studies had been given an important start in France by Richard Simon (1638–1712). After a stormy career Simon died within the church, although he had been expelled by the Oratorians and had scandalized Bishop Bossuet (1627–1704) for having applied the term "critical" to the study of the Bible. Today the *Encyclopedia Catholica* refers to him favorably as "among the pioneers of biblical criticism," yet his contemporaries at the Sorbonne ordered his books burned. The French church of the eighteenth century was unable to see the rise of this historical consciousness as an opportunity but only as a threat. At the very beginning of the century Bossuet had warned of "the intemperance of the mind." Intellectual modernity loomed in his mind as an ominous threat to faith. He wrote prophetically, "I see preparations for a grand assault upon the Church." Clerical intransigence helped make this a self-fulfilling prophecy.

## Philosophy and Piety

A rigid orthodoxy combined with state power dominated the cultural and religious life of Protestant Germany, offering little more encouragement for the emergence of a modern Christianity than that of France. Despite a deep conservatism, eighteenth-century German Protestantism proved more able than Roman Catholicism to respond creatively to the new currents of thought. By the end of the Thirty Years' War there was a restiveness in many quarters with the terrible toll of confessional arrogance when supported at the price of religious wars. Here and there throughout the myriad of German cities, principalities, and states of the eighteenth century were places in which an atmosphere of guarded freedom allowed the growth of a new theology. By 1740, Frederick the Great encouraged the Enlightenment rationalism. He restored the rationalistic philosopher Christian Wolff to his professorship in Halle from which Frederick William I had deposed him at the insistence of the Lutheran pastors. The pastors had convinced their king that rationalism was dangerously subversive to the state. They said Wolff's doctrine of "sufficient reason" undercut loyalty to the state which could only be upheld by religious dogmatism. Frederick II was not convinced by such arguments and allowed professors, statesmen, and all to ponder Wolff's *Philosophical Thoughts on God, the World, and the Human Soul,* as long as such things did not impede the unity and growth of the state.

The decisive intellectual factor in this acceptance of the new science in Germany was the influence of the philosophy of Gottfried Wilhelm von Leibniz (1646–1716). The largely unsystematic work of Leibniz had been organized by Wolff and formed the basis of the general philosophical orientation of the German universities of the eighteenth century. The Leibniz-Wolff philosophy provided a means of integrating Christian faith into the new scientific world view, richer in creative options than the less metaphysical empiricism that dominated English thought. The keynote of the philosophy of Leibniz is inclusiveness. His theory of knowledge, unlike Locke's, was rationalistic rather than purely empirical. However, in theology Leibniz did not wish to limit himself, as Lord Herbert had, to those truths about God which can be reached deductively by the operation of the mind itself. The mind, by its a priori operation, can construct a natural theology. But this natural theology may legitimately be supplemented by the truths of revelation. In his "Discourse over the Conformity of Faith with Reason," he writes:

> I assume that the two truths [i.e., reason and revelation] cannot contradict one another. Faith has to do with the truth God has revealed in an extraordinary way and reason is in the coherence of truths, . . . which the human mind can attain by natural means without the assistance of the light of faith.[1]

Natural theology partook of the nature of necessary truth being derived by application of the law of noncontradiction. "Necessary truths can be demonstrated, that is reduced to identical propositions" through analysis by the human mind. The truths of revelation are "truths of fact" or "contingent truths." Such truths have to be learned through experience, of which revelation is a particular type. The contingent character of the truths of revelation is due to the limited abilities of the human mind.

"Contingent truths require an infinite analysis which can be performed only by God, so that He alone can know them *a priori* and with certainty."[2] Contingent truths are not in some sense less true. In the mind of God they have the same certainty as the necessary truths. The difference is in the means by which men know them.

Leibniz construed the realm of the contingent truths of revelation broadly. He did not feel that the Biblical miracles, the doctrine of the Trinity, or the two natures of Christ were a burden no rational man could bear. In many respects he provided the basis for a very conservative philosophical scheme for unifying reason and revelation. As Zscharnack observed, "The rationalism of the German universities was far removed from the Enlightenment which dominated the courts, the cities and the bourgeoisie."[3] But the next two generations of theologians were to discover that there was an ambiguity at the heart of Leibniz' seemingly happy coordination of reason and revelation.

The reception of modern philosophy and science into German church life was shaped not only by its intellectual atmosphere but also by new forms of spirituality. Well before the intellectual hegemony of Protestant orthodoxy had been shaken by philosophical radicalism, its religious meaning had been attacked. Pietism, as it became known, arose in Germany after the Thirty Years' War as a protest against spiritual barrenness and formalism of the great state churches. Pietism took form under the leadership of Philipp Jakob Spener (1635–1705), who described in his *Pia Desideria* a program of church reform based on the deepening of Christocentric personal piety linked with a renewal of practical Biblical preaching. In contrast to orthodoxy, with its emphasis on the objective forensic act of justification as the center of Christianity, Pietists emphasized the subjective, personal experience of rebirth through a direct experience of Christ. Instead of a theology based on formal syllogism and polemic argument, Pietism held for what Gottfried Arnold (1666–1714) called *Theologia Experimentalis,* that is, a theology growing out of personal experience of Christ and the Bible. Arnold was quite clear in warning that whoever "treats the Scriptures without the Holy Spirit's light and grace, such cannot be helped by the true foundation of apostles and prophets."[4] The born-again man is freed not only from hell but from the power of sin in his life here and now. This newness is expressed through the "fruits of the Spirit," the good works done in joyous obedience to the indwelling of Christ. Spener teaches that we know we are reborn "not by a special direct revelation but by the witness of the fruit, that we obey his commands."[5]

Pietism is a difficult movement to evaluate and relate to the intellectual life of the church. Its piety often degenerated into a lachrymose subjectivism which was castigated by its contemporaries as "unbearably affected." Its spiritual discipline became at times a repressive "methodism like that of the monks." Criticism from the philosophers and theologians of the eighteenth century was unrelenting. Reflecting on his youthful experience with Pietism, Johann Semler said he had seen "few real conversions but many conversions to hypocrisy."[6] Its subjectively oriented exegesis quickly went over into allegorical fantasy. Its emphasis on experience against doctrine often became an excuse for anti-intellectualism. For all these sins the movement was widely castigated in its own time and since. Yet its effect on theology and on the intellectual and artistic life of Germany is undeniable. The key to this contradiction lies in the complexity of Pietism itself. Pietism stands in spirit between Reformation and Enlightenment. With the Reformation it is dominated by the question of man's relation to God. With the Enlightenment it sees this relationship in individualistic terms and in its meaning in practical affairs. Pietism had both a conservative and an *avant-garde* influence. By its religious fervor it held back the advance of a militant atheism. By its individualism and subjectivism it undercut the dominance of church life by the doctrinal systems of orthodoxy. The contradiction between old and new runs through the lives of the pietistic leaders. Count Zinzendorf (1700–1760) pondered in his spiritual life on the wounds of Christ, renewing in his time the passion mysticism of the Middle Ages. Yet he was also a devoted reader of Pierre Bayle's *Critical and Historical Dictionary,* long the darling source book of eighteenth-century unbelief. Johann Albrecht Bengel (1687–1752) instituted modern textual studies of the

New Testament with his publication in 1734 of a Greek text complete with a critical apparatus delineating the variations. Yet he also was concerned with apocalyptic calculations, reckoning that Satan was to be bound for a thousand years beginning in 1836, while fortunately leaving some uncertainty as to just when the end would come.[7] These contradictions, so glaring in retrospect, were held together in these men who lived at this time of transition between the old and the new in religion.

Pietism pointed to a religion that could sit loose to the nicely drawn distinctions of Scholastic theology. This thrust of Pietism is revealed in Arnold's book *Unparteiische Kirchen- und Ketzerhistorie,* 1699–1700 (*An Impartial History of the Churches and Heresy*). As a historian Arnold wished his work to be *unparteiisch* ("impartial"), not tied to the dogmatism of any party. But *unparteiisch* was also understood in a mystical sense to designate true Christianity that transcended the confessions and creeds of the church parties whose doctrinal formulas plagued Christianity since its beginnings. For Arnold, the true spirituality of primitive Christianity is not found in the great churches. Rather, the born-again Christians are a tiny minority often persecuted as heretics by the spiritually indifferent majority that define orthodoxy. The limits of real Christianity are set not by doctrinal standards but by a personal religious experience that is compatible with a variety of intellectual formulations. Such a loosening of Christianity from the increasingly dubious intellectual structures of orthodox dogmatics gave theology a muchneeded freedom to develop its relationships to the new philosophy and science.

## The Time of Turning

Intellectual history is marked by few clear transitions from one era to the next. Such is the case with those theologians who developed the new theology of Protestantism in eighteenth-century Germany. The influence of rationalistic philosophy had already been felt early in the century by theologians of "rational orthodoxy." Johann Franz Buddeus (1667–1729), Matthias Pfaff (1668–1760), and Johann Lorenz von Mosheim (1694–

1755) were of this transitional school. The spirit of rational orthodoxy was caught by Albert Schweitzer. "Here—rationalism surrounds religion without touching it and, like a lake surrounding some ancient castle, mirrors its image with curious refractions."[8] These men approached the claims of reason and history out of their solid acceptance of creedal orthodoxy. Yet, to extend Schweitzer's metaphor, it was not long before the lake of rationalism had started to erode the foundation of the old castle of orthodoxy. By the middle of the century a new and bolder synthesis, reflecting not only a rationalistic philosophy but drawing on the new English thought and the spiritual dynamic of Pietism, started to emerge. This new theological synthesis was the work of the neologians. The neologians did their decisive work in about two generations between 1740–1786. The group is characterized by the "consciousness of standing in a yet incompleted development in which the future generation will transform their own views and formulations to something better and more perfect."[9] The neologians were the first generation of theologians to grasp the temporal—perhaps we could better say temporary—character of their work. They understood theology as an intellectual discipline whose end product is not immutable truth. Rather, theology bears witness to a truth which is itself unchanging but is in conceptions and words that share fully in the changeableness of human existence.

## The Essence of Christianity

Johann Salomo Semler (1725–1791) was the very stereotype of the German university professor. His massive research and writing totaled 171 separate items. His almost legendary learning was unfortunately displayed in a prose style turgid to the point of barbarity. Yet from the time of his accession to the professorship of theology at Halle in 1753 until his death, he exerted a wide influence on one of the most vital generations in German theology. With Semler's work, we have reached "the real end of classical orthodox Protestantism [*Altprotestantismus*], in German evangelical theology."[10] In Semler the isolated beginnings of critical insight and historical knowledge of his

contemporaries were enlarged and integrated into the classical
expression of the neologians. He had grasped, as had many of
his contemporaries, the historically conditioned, contingent
character of all theology. But he was not willing to leave this as
an undocumented intuition. He was committed to the slow, patient work of documenting and completing the newly emerging
picture of the growth of the church's theology.

With Locke and the deists the new philosophical and scientific world view held the critical place in the modernization of
theology. With Semler the situation had changed. The scientific
world view and the categories of modern philosophy were assumed. For Semler the cutting edge for the new theology was
in history rather than in philosophy or science. The great new
fact for theology was the relativization of all doctrinal statement when viewed from the perspective of history. The Socinians, Locke, and the deists had grasped partially the historically
conditioned character of Christian doctrine and even of the New
Testament itself. Yet their work on history was not much more
than a series of well-informed guesses. In the case of Toland
and his acceptance of the spurious *Nazarenus,* his work was
only wishful thinking in support of a markedly nonhistorical
thesis. By the latter half of the eighteenth century, and to no
small extent through the work of Semler himself, a comprehensive picture of this history of dogma was becoming a reality.
Men were no longer forced to study dogma only theologically.
Now it could be studied historically to reveal the intellectual,
religious, political, and social forces that shaped it. The future
of theology was not to be shaped by the efforts to overcome
dogma by still more dogma as had been the pattern of polemic
theology, both Catholic and Protestant. Now men could overcome dogma by history. The tyranny of an inadequate dogma
could be overcome by historical analysis that pointed beyond
the dogma to the underlying realities to which it had once borne
witness.

Semler recognized that Christianity had developed from the
time of its inception into a complex system of thought and institutions. The cultural complex of Christendom had much in it
that was not part of original revelation but a product of the

interaction of Christianity with various cultures. As the faith spread through the world, "Christian colonies" were formed, each of which developed its own form of doctrine.[11] This interaction between Christian faith and the world was good and necessary. Without it there could have been no Christian mission. But, as Semler perceived, this interaction has another meaning, overlooked by the theology of the time. There can be no neat equation between revelation and any of the particular theologies developed in the Christian colonies. Theology is a product of its time and place. It cannot share the claim to universal validity with revelation. Even by retreating to Scripture itself there is no escape from the relativities of history. "Holy Scripture and the Word of God are to be very clearly differentiated. . . . To the Holy Scriptures, as they have been given particular historical expression among the Jews, belong Ruth, Esther and the Song of Songs etc., but these so called Holy Books do not at all belong to the Word of God, which gives salvation to all men in all time."[12] Nor is Semler willing to provide a sanctuary by turning to the New Testament alone. Even New Testament Scripture provides "no record or registry of only perfectly legitimate ideas."[13]

The future for theology, Semler believed, was not in trying to claim infallibility for any system of doctrine. Rather, the search must be made for the center of religious truth and vitality within all the various doctrinal forms of Christendom. There is a creative center or "essence" that forms the basis of every theology. By assuming the identity of the religion of Jesus with natural religion the deists were able to effect a number of crucial distinctions between primitive Christianity and the creedal orthodoxy of later centuries. But their conception of essence was far too narrow and rationalistic to provide an adequate account of the growth of dogma. Semler was not willing to admit that the essence could be reduced to doctrinal statements. Was not the creative center of Christian faith in the personal relation of the believer with God, rather than in any formulas?

The unadmitted assumption that had linked the most radical deist and the most fervently conservative orthodox theologian was belief in the definition of religion through verbal formulas.

It was just this assumption which Semler was placing under critical examination. Semler's oft-despised pietistic upbringing had given him a perspective on theology found neither in orthodoxy nor in rationalism. Faith does not live simply in the intellect. There is something about religious faith, Semler contended, which does not allow it to be treated adequately in intellectual terms or measured by objective, absolute standards.[14] The creative center of Christian faith is in man's relation to God. He uses the term "the moral worship of God" to characterize this dynamic essence of Christianity. Semler can be easily misunderstood at this point. The moral worship of God does not mean the reduction of Christian faith to a simple moralistic religion. "Moral" for Semler is synonymous with "ethical-religious" or even "personal-spiritual," rather than simply "legal-judgmental." The true opposite to "moral" is "physical." In characterizing different ways of understanding man's relation to God, Semler contrasts the "magical-sacramental" conceptions as physical with the moral that is distinctive of Christianity. To borrow a twentieth-century distinction to explain an eighteenth-century theologian, the moral relationship to God implies what Buber meant in speaking of an "I–Thou" in contrast to an "I–it" relationship. There is in the moral worship of God a quality springing from its personal-spiritual aspects that eludes codification.

Semler sharpens his meaning by the distinction he draws between public and private religion. The essence of Christianity lies in the private religion of the individual believer. "Christ is the Author of the uniquely free private religion of all Christians."[15] As religious fellowships come into being the necessity arises for some public expression of the unique faith that animates the group. There is a public religion which by its very nature must define itself through verbal formulas and institutional forms. Without such definitions there would be only chaos. Historically the public religion of Christians was characterized by the definition of the doctrines of the Trinity, the two natures, atonement, etc. All these public definitions of Christian faith share in the particularity of their time and place. For this reason public religion can claim neither finality nor infallibility for itself, nor can it be set up as a norm for private religion. The private religion of the Christian is "uniquely free" because it is the personal response to God's revelation given historically in Christ and now imparted by the Holy Spirit.

Orthodoxy had always argued vigorously against any relativizing of standards. The supposedly inescapable paradox for Christianity was: Creed or Chaos. Semler simply refused to accept this paradox. Although rejecting absolutism, he was not refusing to judge theological statements. He rejects the legal-objective conception of heresy but puts in its place a functional or practical view. The crucial question about any doctrinal formulation is how it functions in the life of the believer. Does the public doctrine of a particular Christian fellowship hinder or help the moral and spiritual life of its members? With Semler the pietistic, practical expression of religion has taken its place as the criterion for theology. The real touchstone for the reality of God is not a formula but growth in the life of grace. Doctrine is heretical when it keeps people from fulfilling the divine will in love. Emphasis on the private faith of the Christian did not make Semler a prophet of "religionless Christianity." He believed that public religion had an essential place in Christianity. He was never in sympathy with the Enlightenment radicals who wanted to make sweeping changes in liturgy, creeds, and hymns to rid them of crass or irrational religious ideas. The religious life of those on a lower intellectual or cultural level must be taken into account. To rob people of a familiar and fruitful religious form in the interest of some abstract notion of rationality would be wrong. Religion had to retain its popular forms in order to support the social order and guide the moral life of the people.

Judging theological doctrine by practical criteria leads to a new attitude toward doctrinal controversy. No longer is fanatic self-righteousness a possibility. In the face of doctrinal conflict the stance of the Christian is openness and freedom. To all doctrinal statements "the conscience of the Christian stands entirely free."[16] The stance of the theologian must be one of liberalism. Semler's liberalism did not mean a particular set of theological ideas as was later to be the case. Instead, it was an attitude of freedom or, as Hirsch suggests, "broadmindedness" or "large-heartedness" (*weitherzig*).[17] Semler gives the first hint of the term "liberal theology" in the title of the Latin edition of his systematic theology: *Institutio ad doctrinam Christianem liberaliter discendem* (1774), and of "liberal interpretation" of Scripture in his *Amparatus ad liberalem Novi Testamenti interpretationem* (1767). For Semler such liberalism did not spring from indifference, nor did he feel it a concession to be made by theology as it moved on to full-blown rationalism. His liberalism had deeply religious roots and developed as a corollary of his pietistic conception of how personal religion and doctrine are related. The conscience of the believer stands free to the formulas of public religion finally because the reality of God is found in personal relation to God, not in dubious claims to knowledge about the inner workings of the Trinity or the being of Christ. Liberalism for Semler was the fruit of humility before the greatness of God and the limitations of our knowledge. Semler proposed that such a liberalism be made a part of all theological thinking.

## Christology in Tension

The dual commitment of the neologians to Christian faith in its churchly expressions and to the modern world led them into a dilemma from which they never really escaped. In their search for the essentials of the Christian faith they had sundered apart what had long been together. The Trinitarian form was retained, but any doctrine of the relationship of the members was rejected. The doctrine of the two natures of Christ was retained, but opinions about how the natures related were rejected as dangerously divisive. The death of Christ was the key to salvation, but the substitutionary doctrine of the atonement was ethically ill-founded. The question the neologians posed in their Christology was whether traditional doctrine could be retained as a general set of affirmations while cutting away from it the vast substructure of theological teaching that had so long supported it.

The contrast between Semler and the deists can be seen in his analysis of the three favorite themes of the Lockean Christology: Messiahship, miracle, and prophecy. Semler accepted and extended the deists' work of dismantling the verification scheme suggested by Locke. Yet he did not believe that historical studies of Messiahship, miracle, and prophecy really touched the central issues in Christology. Messiahship is no longer the crucial characterization of Jesus. Its importance was only in its usefulness in communicating with the ancient Jews. Similarly, the proof from miracles was cast aside as unessential, not because of the problem of historicity, but because of the unsuitability of miracle to prove the mission of Jesus. The proof from miracle belongs only to the infancy of Christianity. Miracle and fulfilled prophecy were "the first step to Christianity." Such proof was appropriate to the ancient Jews, Semler contended, because they could only believe in salvation coming through miraculous events. The Jewish expectations for the coming Kingdom were for a this-worldly, sensual salvation. Such changes require a physical miracle. So it was very natural that belief in miracle was a part of early Christianity. With the removal of Christianity from the inadequate mythological world view of Judaism, miracle was no longer an essential part of Christological thinking. The miracle doctrine was but an inadequate "clothing" (*Einkleidung*) with which Christianity was invested in its infancy. It had already shed this doctrine during the lifetime of the apostles, who do not mention it again in the epistles.[18] There is no need in the present to be encumbered with the inadequacies of the past.

The argument from fulfilled prophecy was rejected because of its theological impossibility rather than simply out of an awareness of the historical and exegetical difficulties that attend it. Strictly speaking, a prophecy of Christ is a contradiction in terms. The true meaning of Messiahship remained a mystery until revealed by Christ. The "universal, moral meaning" of Messiahship given by Jesus is "a new teaching, a new advance in knowledge" which could not be prophesied because the Old Testament prophets still stood within the particularism of Judaism.[19] The newness of Christ's revelation is its universality and power to effect moral change. Verification comes in the experience of the believer living in faith. Questions of the historicity of miracle and accuracy of prophecy have no power to bind the Christian conscience. Historical analysis can work in complete freedom. Believers may have a perfectly sound Christian faith and nevertheless "leave these stories aside because they are too opaque for them."[20]

Semler rejected Locke's definition of the essence of Christianity—Jesus is the Messiah—in favor of a Trinitarian confession reinterpreted along personal, ethical lines.

> To love God with the whole heart, with all the powers of the soul, and to have faith in his Son and the Holy Spirit, and then according to the doctrine of the Son to love the neighbor as the self, this is the sole, true, active religion of the Christians.[21]

For Semler the Trinitarian form of the confession is as essential as its practical orientation. Neither the simple monotheism of the ancient Hebrews nor the philosophically sophisticated God of deism is the God of Christian faith. Trinitarianism is in essence "a threefold moral proclamation" about God and how he works for human salvation.[22] This proclamation brings together the whole meaning of Christian faith: Christianity is a faith in the one God and Father of all men, in Jesus Christ as the divinely empowered teacher, benefactor, and Savior, who taught the universal love of God for all men in contradiction to the errors of Jews and heathens, and in the Holy Spirit, who still imparts the doctrines of Jesus to believers and awakens in them a new and higher form of life.

The center of the Trinitarian confession is the revelation in Christ. He is the one who reveals God as gracious and worthy of love rather than fear.[23] Through his life and teachings Jesus shows the universality of God's love in distinction to the nationalistic particularism that infected the religions of antiquity. Now the Holy Spirit continues to reveal Jesus' doctrine and produce in the believer a higher form of spiritual life. Hence, to speak of God as Father, Son, and Spirit is to say that all of man's spiritual life is dependent on God. The joining together of

Father, Son, and Spirit is the only adequate means of expressing all that is integral to the proper worship of God. However, every attempt to change the Trinitarian confession into an exact description of the inner life of God falls into the category of unessential teaching, especially when such teaching is the source of party strife. To these the Christian conscience is entirely free.

The doctrine of the divine and human natures of Christ is given moral and historical analysis similar to that given the Trinity. Semler's redefinition shifts the basis for considering the divinity of Christ. He moves away from a doctrine of the being of Christ to a doctrine of revelation through Christ. Belief in the divinity of Christ is the faith that in him God was revealing a new way to salvation. This doctrine distinguishes Christianity from the deists, who hold that the message of Jesus is but the "republication" of truths knowable by unaided human reason. Although the revelation in Christ in no way contradicts reason, it is nonetheless unique. Through Jesus Christ man can encounter the reality of God as in no other person. To confess this is to believe in the divinity of Christ. The doctrine of the divinity of Christ has been badly misunderstood at times by the church. The source of this misunderstanding was the tendency to conceive of the divine nature in metaphysical rather than in moral terms. Describing Christ's nature in metaphysical terms leads to a "sensuous" or "natural" conception of his divinity. The divine presence is construed in terms of Christ's having supernatural qualities such as omnipotence, omniscience, and omnipresence. The moral redemption brought by Christ, Semler contends, is not based on his having these qualities which are only needed to explain a sensuous or "this-worldly" salvation. The true miracle of Christ is his power to bring the believer into a new and higher level of spiritual life.

Behind all the arguments of orthodoxy about Christ's divinity stands the conviction that if his divinity were in any sense incomplete, he could not be Savior. This line of argumentation had been introduced by Athanasius in his battle against Arianism and had dominated Christological thinking ever since. Semler proposed to stand this argument on its head. Inadequate conceptions of Christ's humanity endanger his Saviorhood. The orthodox doctrine of the two natures of Christ certainly supports Semler in this contention. He need not be feared as a heretic at this point. However, he is saying something more radical than this. Despite the formal acceptance of full humanity, the metaphysical doctrine of Christ's divinity used by the orthodox teachers does, in fact, endanger the reality of the human nature. Modern Christology has accepted Semler's critique and consistently upbraided traditional orthodoxy for its potential if not actual Docetism. For Christ to be the Saviour of men he must have been a real man, no matter what else we say about him. Semler wanted to go beyond insisting that Jesus had a physical being like our own. Human nature means Jesus' complete involvement in the human condition. "Christ has freely stepped into the moral situation and relationships of men."[24] The force of Jesus' ethical teachings stem from his real humanity. Any interpretation that overshadows his humanity with divinity is to be rejected because it makes him irrelevant to the moral struggles of man from which Christ alone can deliver.

## Atonement and Ethics

The tension between Christian doctrine and the spirit of the Enlightenment was at no point more acute than in the doctrine of the atonement. Throughout history Christian faith has used a variety of symbols and metaphors to describe the divine-human reconciliation. The thinkers of the Enlightenment period did not see this richness and variety. They tended to understand the Christian doctrine of reconciliation in terms of the doctrine of substitutionary atonement as elaborated by Protestant orthodox theology. The neologians were confronted with what had become a *cause célèbre* among the rationalistic critics of Christianity. Put in its boldest terms the individualistic, rationalistic ethic of the Enlightenment had no place in it for any doctrine of substitutionary atonement. On strictly legal grounds—and for the Enlightenment no one was more law-abiding than God—no one can assume the punishment due another. Punishment for sins is due each person in direct proportion to the severity of the sins. In this light, how can a moral God be satisfied with the sufferings of an innocent Christ to atone for the sins of other men? Yet it was just such an enormity, the Enlightenment radicals said, that the church was fastening on God.

The basis of Semler's doctrine of reconciliation is his analysis of the New Testament concepts. He was aware of a tremendous conceptual revolution taking place in the first-century Christian communities. The early Christians were developing "a new language" to explain what God had done in Christ for the salvation of man. Like every such language it displayed its relationship to its time. "The first new language of the Christians is still half-Jewish."[25] This language turned naturally and inevitably to the metaphors of sacrifice as the key to redemption. "But these old expressions and idioms now receive an ever greater content when the Christian uses them."[26] The key to finding this "greater content" lies in the way in which the New Testament writers use the imagery of sacrifice drawn from the Old. There is one important difference between Old and New Testament use of the sacrificial idea. The sacrifice of Jesus is not simply one sacrificial death in a continuing series. It is the final and perfect sacrifice. Christ is the last priest, the cross the last altar, and Jesus himself the last and perfect sacrifice. By his death he had opened a "new and living way" to God (Heb. 10:20). The way to God is no longer controlled by one priesthood or limited to one people. It is this universal love that brings reconciliation, rather than the sufferings and death of Christ. For Semler the restructuring of the sacrificial idea in the New Testament marked the end of sacrifice in a literal sense. The inner meaning of sacrificial language is that reconciliation is universal. It is possible not because Jesus died but because he revealed in his death God's universal love.

In Semler's historical analysis of atonement doctrine the notion of a ransom to Satan was easily seen as a concession to the mythological world view. The crucial theologian was Anselm, whose atonement doctrine opened the way to the distinctive developments of the legal substitution doctrine of Protestant orthodoxy. Semler realized that to get involved in the details of Anselm's arguments about the merits of Christ would be to accept Anselm's presupposition. Instead, he asks the meaning of Anselm's theory of atonement in its broadest terms. To say that Christ takes over the punishment due to men for their sins, Semler argues, is another way of saying that God deals with men graciously. God does not make us suffer an exact equivalence for our sins. This does not mean that men do not suffer at all for their sins. Some suffering has the important effect of improving the character of the sinner. But God's punishment has as its purpose reformation of character, not satisfaction of the divine wrath. God is willing to give anyone, no matter how horrendous his sins, a new start in life when he turns from his old ways in repentance and faith. Semler sums up his historical analysis of atonement doctrine: "In all these kinds of language [i.e., atonement doctrines] there is expressed a conception of Christ from which comes this result: all men can equally well assure themselves of the love of God."[27]

The universality of the love of God leads to the second motif in atonement doctrine: Christ revealed the basis of man's relationship to God as purely moral. The new relationship of Sonship which God had opened through Christ is universal in scope precisely because it is based upon the moral law.[28] Semler sees the religions of the world in two groups: there are the ritualistic-particularistic religions, like Judaism, and the heathen religions of antiquity. These religions base man's relation to God on ritual acts done by a special priesthood and, hence, by their very nature, are particularistic. Christianity is moral-universal in character. The new relation to God given by Christ brings about change in human life. The love of God is born in human hearts and enables men to live in fuller obedience. This "moral worship of God" comes uniquely through Christ.

> Whoever knows Christ as a Mirror and Teacher of the divine goodness and kindness, who through this view of him, or faith in him, kindles a love of God in the mind of the sinner, that person has the best knowledge of Christ.[29]

Semler is not teaching a legalistic perfectionism. Jesus is not simply a moral example. God does not await moral perfection before accepting men into fellowship with himself. The critical determinant is the beginning of moral growth through repentance and faith.

In the traditional doctrine of atonement and justification the merits of Christ provide the basis on which a sinner is declared just in the sight of God. Man is given a status—that of a just man—which he does not possess in his own right. Man is still a sinner. His acceptance by God is created by the imputing to him of the righteousness of Christ. Semler was wary of such teaching because it too easily degenerated into a doctrine of "cheap grace." He set about wrestling with the paradox that has always bedeviled justification doctrine from its beginnings. If men are accepted by God solely through the merits of Christ, can they not then pursue their lives of sinfulness? Paul saw the problem already in the first century in his letter to the Romans: "Where sin increased, grace abounded all the more. . . . What shall we say then? Are we to continue in sin that grace may abound?" Paul's answer was simple and direct, if not theoretically satisfying: "By no means!" (Rom. 5:20; 6:1–2.) In his *Versuch einer freiern theologischen Lehrart,* Semler draws on the thought of Richard Baxter (1615–1691), the English Puritan who had been translated into German by Spener. The puritan theology had recognized the importance for a  proper doctrine of reconciliation of holding together the objective reality of what God had done in Christ with its subjective appropriation in the life of the believer. Baxter described the objective side of reconciliation in terms of substitutionary atonement. Semler saw the objective aspects in the revelation of a truly universal, moral religion of Christ. They are at one in understanding the need for personal appropriation of the grace of God. There could be no true justification without a change in life. Yet in saying this Semler does not want to reject Luther's picture of the Christian man "as a sinner yet just." God does accept men while the power of sin still remains in their lives. It is not man's present moral status but his direction of life that is vital. If a sinner has turned to God in repentance and faith, he has started on a spiritual growth that will eventually render him acceptable. Repentance and faith do not produce instantaneous perfection. They start a moral growth that in the providence of God can go to perfection in eternity.

There remains one crucial question. What function does Jesus, particularly in his death on the cross, have in awakening in men the response of loving obedience to the law of God? In answering this Semler goes to the very heart of orthodox atonement doctrine—the idea of substitution. He seemingly teeters on the edge of accepting an idea he had rejected.

> Christ has freely stepped into the moral situation and relationships of men, taking upon himself, their total obligation within which he perfectly fulfilled the law of God in all its fullness in whatever particular circumstances he went. . . . He let guilt be reckoned to himself, and took over all punishments which were due as the results of the sins of particular men.[30]

The crucial turn in his thinking comes in determining the exact function of the sufferings of Christ.

> In the sufferings of Christ, as sufferings, God has no satisfaction, and one must not reckon the worth of the satisfaction from the size of the punishment, but the solely correct ground whereby its worth is to be reckoned was the unique aptitude of this humiliation of Christ in reaching the end purpose of punishment in the wise and just government of God.[31]

The end purposes of the punishment are "to indicate the hatred of God against sin, to bring men to the place that they want to obey his law out of love itself; that others would be frightened away from further sins, the common good among men be advanced and the true honor of the *justitiae rectricis* be saved." By his willing acceptance of the humiliation, suffering, and death for others, Christ inspires in men a response of obedience not for any reward but "out of love itself." What is changed by Christ's free acceptance of suffering and death is not God's attitude toward sinners. This has always been one of grace. What is changed is the sinner. He is turned in repentance and faith away from his sins to a life of moral growth.

Semler is difficult to interpret at this point. He is struggling to give expression to a basic Christian truth to which no type of language was ever really adequate. It was a truth to which the language of the Enlightenment was uniquely ill-suited. To speak of Jesus as the "moral Lord" implies far more than

simply that Jesus was a great ethical example or teacher. This is true but inadequate. By his free acceptance of suffering and death for others he was lifted above the status of mere example. He is a Savior. He is the source of an inner transformation of human personality. Semler knew that the problem of human motivation did not resolve itself simply into the need for moral knowledge. This he saw was the weakness of the deists. What was needed was a transformation that could give the world "new men." Such change comes from faith in Christ. This is what it means to confess him as moral Lord.

## Chapter VII

# ALL THE WAY

# WITH REASON

### The Religion About Christ—The Religion of Christ

There seemed to be an almost irresistible inner logic at work in eighteenth-century theology, forcing it into increasingly rationalistic forms. The neologians had been no more able than the deists before them to establish the proper critical relation between revelation and reason, so natural religion had become a Procrustean bed shortening Christian faith to its own dimensions. The thoroughgoing rationalists who succeeded the neologians by the end of the eighteenth century saw this development as natural and necessary. Heinrich P. K. Henke (1752–1809), one of the pioneers of thoroughgoing rationalism, gave classic expression to their views: "Every revealed religion goes over gradually into a rational one, and man can with this elevate himself, so that he finds in the instruction given through another human being no longer the benefit of the source of truth but only the channel, not of the light itself, but only the lamp."[1] It has been the penchant of later interpreters to see the advance of rationalism in theology as the intrusion of an alien and destructive force into the intellectual life of the church. Such was not the view of the rationalists themselves. They believed that with rationalism, Christianity had moved to a new and higher stage of its development. Rational religion is not alien to Christianity because reason speaks with the voice of God himself

128

Heinrich Eberhard Gottlob Paulus (1761–1851), the famous rationalistic theologian of Heidelberg, could speak confidently of "the biblical Christian rationalism."

Henke speaks in opposition to what he termed "Christolatry" of the rendering to Jesus a worship due only to God. In a phrase that was to become a classic of religious liberalism, he asserts that the true honor of Jesus comes in replacing "the religion about Christ with the religion of Christ." The rationalistic critique left Christology, as such, without a subject matter. Johann Friedrich Röhr (1777–1848) said that the doctrine of the person and work of Christ was not a part of religion as such. It is to be replaced by the teachings and example of Christ. In his *Lineamenta,* Henke makes Christology a subdivision of anthropology. The doctrine of the two natures had been swallowed up in the full humanity of Jesus. All assertions of the divinity of Christ can be reduced to one: Jesus Christ was a man entrusted by divine providence with the historical task of establishing a universal religion based on the ethical-religious truths vouchsafed to man by reason and conscience. The uniqueness of Christ is not explained in terms of his being of one substance with the Father. Christ is unique because of the special place he holds in the divine providence. This was the factor that allowed him to carry out his work. Jesus' work of liberation of religion from superstition and particularism was not complete in his own life. It was still necessary for rationalistic analysis to complete the freeing of true religion from the husks that an erring and ignorant humanity had placed about it. "From being surrounded by limitations and coverings, the seed of life-giving truth grew until it burst forth to be completely self-evident."[2]

The historical proofs of Christ's divinity through fulfilled prophecy and miracles were no longer necessary since his divinity, as such, was not an object of belief. Biblical history was not a means of validating the faith but an embarrassment needing explanation. Just how could Jesus the teacher of rational religion have been associated with the obviously irrational notions of eschatology or with the miracle stories of the New Testament? Part of the answer is simple. Jesus had accommodated himself to the "superstitions of the Jews." Henke argues that the only form within which the Jews were able to conceive a liberator sent from God was in terms of their messianic hope. Jesus utilized this hope but showed the falseness of the nationalistic messianic ideal by his refusal to fulfill it. He pointed the people by this frustration beyond the limitations of their messianism to something higher—a moral conception of Messiahship.

It was fairly easy to "spiritualize" eschatology or view it as an accommodation. But how is it possible to account for Jesus as a miracle worker? In his *Life of Jesus,* Paulus gives answer. The miracles are seen in the New Testament as historical events because this is what people of the first century believed had happened. Jesus' contemporaries perceived certain events as direct divine intervention in which the laws of nature were superseded. Men perceived these so-called miracles in this way because they were ignorant of the natural causes actually at work. Only as modern science made men aware of the causal nexus of events were miracles seen for what they are. Paulus had uncovered in this observation a fact of basic importance for historical understanding. Perception of events is historically conditioned by the culture of which we are a part. Men in the ancient world did not see reality as a law-abiding mechanism in which event is causally related to antecedent events. Rather, the world was the scene of supernatural activity. In such a perspective an unusual event was judged supernatural without any effort to ascertain a natural explanation. Paulus took this perfectly valid insight and made it the basis for an all-embracing explanation of the New Testament miracles. By a kind of tour de force, he lifts the miracles out of their setting in first-century literature and reinterprets them in the light of eighteenth-century science. The outcome is a work of amazing ingenuity. Everything can be explained, given the will to explain it. Jesus' walking on the water was simply a mistake in perception by the disciples. What they really saw was Jesus walking along the shore on a foggy day. The feeding miracles involved no multiplication of loaves and fishes. The generosity of a small boy in sharing his food led others to share theirs. Many of the healing miracles involved materia medica. The healing of the man born blind (John 9:1–12) was the result of anointing the man's eyes with clay. People jumped to the wrong conclusion "because the medical remedy is so incompletely described that the healing must have been supernatural."[3] A fuller report would have revealed the event to be purely natural. Many of the healings were explained as illustrations of the power of spirit over the human nervous system—an explanation still cherished by many to this day. Paulus was greatly impressed with the power of spirit over body. The eighteenth century was very much alive to the pseudo-scientific theories of Mesmer about "animal magnetism" and the influence of mind over matter. With what seems a surprising inconsistency to the naturalism of the twentieth century, Paulus even undertakes an explanation of the virgin birth. He implies that Jesus was not the issue of a normal sexual union but "that the begetting of the great Son would be the result of a holy inspiration and a power worthy of God."[4]

The crucifixion and resurrection narratives were the center of the challenge to rationalism. The New Testament clearly teaches that Jesus lived again after his crucifixion. How is this possible? The answer is not far to seek. Jesus, in fact, never really died. When taken from the cross he was in a deep swoon. Within the providence of God the sufferings of Jesus in the crucifixion were of such a nature as to render resuscitation a possibility. The key for Paulus' explanation is the spear wound Jesus received in his side. According to the Johannine report (John 19:34), Jesus received this blow after he was supposedly dead. The wound resulted in the discharge of blood and body fluid. This is, in itself, evidence that Jesus was not dead, although "he bowed his head and gave up his spirit." The function of this wound was to release the pressure of body fluid against the heart and lungs which would otherwise have proved fatal. Jesus' actual return to consciousness may have resulted from the aromatic spices used to embalm him. But Paulus puts forward another suggestion informed by the latest scientific discoveries. By reflection on Galvani's work on the effect of electricity on the neuromuscular system, plus a little fantasy, Paulus suggests that Jesus was stimulated back to consciousness by electrical waves generated in a lightning storm. This particular lightning storm had been associated with the earthquake that rolled the stone from the grave. The resuscitated Jesus then left the tomb.

Dropping off the gravecloths, he provided himself with the garments of a gardener. This unaccustomed clothing created some confusion for Mary when she met Jesus. But his identity was soon established by the disciples.

The durability of the resuscitation theory of resurrection is itself amazing. It has become a standard item in rationalistic lives of Jesus down to the present. The theory can be given a very uncomplimentary twist as Paulus anticipated. It could be argued that the whole affair was staged by Jesus as a trick. In a present-day variation Hugh Schonfield argues that Jesus had made careful preparations to stage an apparent death followed by a bodily resurrection. "A conspiracy had to be organized of which the victim himself was the deliberate secret instigator. It was a nightmarish conception and undertaking, the outcome of the frightening logic of a sick mind, or of a genius. And it worked out."[5] Paulus would have nothing of such a notion. Jesus' death was not staged with an eye to resuscitation. People believed him genuinely dead. Resurrection was the result of the confluence of a number of happy providences—the apparent death, the spear wound, the aromatic spices, the electrical storm, and the earthquake. No one of these broke the law of nature. But their coming together provided a striking event to verify to Jesus' contemporaries the great truths he was teaching.

Paulus presents none of his explanations as final. He said repeatedly that he did not want to be remembered for them. Yet this has been his fate. His concern with the miracle stories was twofold. First, physical miracles are impossible because of the divinely established order of nature. Unlike Newton and Locke, or even Semler, Paulus did not see the order of nature as something God could command at will. The violation of such laws would be the violation of the divine nature. The Gospel writers intended to relate miracles, it is true. They did this because this was the way in which they perceived these happenings. Rationalistic explanation in no way impugns the honesty of these writers. Explanations are only made in recognition of the differing conceptions of reality in the first century and in the modern world. Second, by putting the physical miracles in their proper light, it is possible to focus on the true miracle of Jesus' ministry. This is the miracle of his purity and the holiness of his character which is so uniquely suited for imitation by mankind as a whole.

Gone for the thoroughgoing rationalist were those agonizing reappraisals of atonement doctrine to find some saving vestige of truth amid an idea rejected from the start. The saving power of Christ was in the force of his teachings and the nobility of his example.

> What then was original but that which has effected the most far advanced peoples of the earth? Yet it appears so simple, so free of dogma and opinionated teachings, so free of every technical term, so necessary and feasible a challenge to the wills of the uncultured as to those of the highest culture. In all time and all places, it really causes an honest, active creation of justice in the mind, the bettering of outward circumstances and can make the human spirit harmonious and well pleasing to God.[6]

Such is the spirit of Jesus which directs the true Christian who "thinks upon, believes and follows the pathway of the Exemplar." There is about Jesus more than the dull gray mantle of pedestrian virtue. There is still the glow of excitement as we look at the ennobling example of this "life which short as it was changed the course of the ages." Yet nothing must create the impression that Jesus was a fanatic or a romantic visionary. Paulus sternly warns, "Whatever judgment of belief that does not proceed from reason and understanding, from idea and concept, cannot be protected from superstition."[7] The virtues Jesus taught are solidly rational. The "disciples" become in Paulus' interpretation "pupils," and their "faith" becomes "sincerity of conviction." A belief willfully held against the evidence of reason is not capable of changing human behavior. Such beliefs are not suitable to the high and difficult task of Christian living because they change as easily as does the will.

## The Practical Impact of Pure Reason

Thoroughgoing rationalism only served to deepen the resistance of conservative churchmen to the new movements in theology. As an apologetic, thoroughgoing rationalism had little to add. By the time it became dominant in theology it had lost its dominance in philosophy. The romantic revolt was under way when Paulus, Henke, Röhr, and Bretschneider were doing their work. Schleiermacher set the new style for apologetics with the religious romanticism of his *Speeches on Religion,* which appeared in 1799, a year before Paulus' first commentaries. Nor was rationalism any more effective in its impact on the practical religious life of the churches. The rationalists shared in the theory that had animated the modernizers of theology from Erasmus onward. To free Christ of the shackles of outworn dogmas was to make him relevant not only to the modern intellectual but also to the unlettered who had long been bemused and repelled by orthodoxy. Thus ran the theory. The facts proved otherwise. The rationalists' revision of liturgy and the pedantic moralism of their sermons numbed and repelled the common man far more than attracted him. A revision of the Lord's Prayer for a rationalistic liturgy illustrates the difficulties:

> Most high Father, let it be our supreme purpose to glorify thee, let truth thrive among us, let virtue already dwell here as it does in heaven. Reward our industry with bread and our forgiving disposition with grace. From severe conflicts preserve us. And finally let all evil cease. That thou are powerful, wise and good over all—let this be our confidence.[8]

The rationalists believed that the wellspring of the moral and spiritual life is in the mind. They failed to grasp the emotional impact of what Paulus stigmatized as "wilful beliefs" on the life of Western man. Man's coming of age was still only a reality for a small intellectual minority. Popular religious life continued to live out of the traditional doctrines and forms. The real legacy of thoroughgoing rationalism was the final liberation of Biblical historical scholarship from doctrinal structures. Rationalism transformed Christology into the study of the life of Jesus. To know the truth about Christ was no longer a matter of the doctrines of the Trinity or the two natures, even in extensively reinterpreted form. Truth was in the teachings and example of Jesus as found by the hardheaded search for historical facticity.

Paulus had grasped the most basic problem in the search for historical facticity—the profound differences in the perception of reality that separate modern men from those of the past. He started to plumb the depths of historical relativism.

It is not enough to say men live in time and must conceive all things historically. Historical relativism means that time and history are in men, shaping the way they perceive themselves and their world. The particularity of the space and time in which we live is not something apart from our inmost being. The complex of values and ideas in which we live shapes us and our perceptions. Paulus caught this vision. But having caught it, he withdrew in horror of the confusion with which it threatened Christianity. His retreat was to the certainties of natural religion rationally perceived. Having found certainty in natural religion, Paulus did not want to scuttle the New Testament as a historical record. So he turned to the rationalization of the New Testament. The New Testament did not contain myth or cunningly contrived legend. It contained history, inadequately perceived. Behind the sophistication of Paulus' rationalism stands a pietistic Biblicism able to find the Word of God speaking directly from each page of Scripture. For Paulus all that had to be done was to set straight the misconceptions of the earlier historians. The inadequacy of his conceptual tools was grasped by David Friedrich Strauss (1808–1874) who passed a telling judgment on thoroughgoing rationalism in theology.

> The insufficiency of the rationalistic system is that it does not perform what is demanded from every system of religious doctrine: namely, first, to give adequate expression to the faith which is the object of the doctrine; and secondly, to place this expression in a relation, whether positive or negative, to science.[9]

Strauss showed that the rationalistic search for facticity involved an appreciation for myth and symbol in religion. Without such an awareness rationalism was betrayed into a non-historical counterfeit of the truth.

*Chapter VIII*

# THE QUESTION
# OF FUNDAMENTALS

## The History of Secondary Causes

With a "grave and temperate irony," Edward Gibbon starts his treatment of the church in *The Decline and Fall of the Roman Empire* with the bland assurance that Christianity had been triumphant "owing to the convincing evidence of the doctrine itself, and to the ruling providence of its great Author." Then he hastens to the matter really at hand.

> But as truth and reason seldom find so favorable a reception in the world, and as the wisdom of Providence frequently condescends to use the passions of the human heart, . . . we may still be permitted . . . to ask, not indeed what was the first, but what were the secondary causes of the rapid growth of the Christian Church.[1]

By the eighteenth century, theologians had pretty well made their peace with the necessity of tracing "secondary causes" in the natural order. But tracing secondary causes in the history of the church and the Bible was causing increasing difficulty. Gibbon's exposé of uncritical credulity, idle superstition, and deliberate deception in the history of Christianity caused a flurry of popular resentment when he made them known to the Englishmen of his day. Since the seventeenth century some in-

tellectuals had known that many of the doctrines of the church
had been wrought in councils swayed by the profane passions
of earthly rulers. Now Gibbon gave this notion public and
piquant statement in his analysis of Nicaea.

> Such was the rise and progress, and such were the natural
> revolutions, of these theological disputes which disturbed the
> peace of Christianity under the reigns of Constantine and of
> his sons. But as those princes presumed to extend their des-
> potism over the faith, . . . the weight of their sufferage some-
> times inclined the ecclesiastical balance: and the prerogatives
> of the King of Heaven were settled, or changed, or modified,
> in the cabinet of an earthly monarch.[2]

Protestants had a ready-made response to any such insinuations
about the church. It was clear that the papal church had been
ridden by all the vices the critical historians displayed. They
did not fear what church history told about the development of
doctrine because all doctrine was supposedly based on the
Bible alone. Although sometimes reluctant about applying historical investigation, Protestantism had in principle the basis
for a thoroughgoing radicalism in its investigation of the church.
Protestantism was based solely upon the authority of Scripture.
As Chillingworth says, "The Bible, the Bible alone is the religion of Protestants." The question remained, Just how open
was Protestantism to a thoroughgoing historicism in the treatment of Scripture? Semler's *Free Investigation of the Canon*
was a good start. But as Lessing suggested, what was needed
now was *A Still Freer Investigation of the Canon of the Old and
New Testaments.*

Awareness of the historically conditioned character of the
Bible brought a slow but persistent attrition in its use as a norm
for theology. This development was fast reaching a limit. If,
under the scrutiny of historical analysis, the figure of Jesus
himself proved to be involved in the intellectual and moral
limitations of his age, then the claim to revelation in him would
be threatened. When in the New Testament Jesus was pictured as
preaching some supposed irrationalism, we are assured that he
was speaking in accommodation to the limitations of his con-

temporaries. Jesus was supposedly conscious of the moral and intellectual limitations of the Jewish-apocalyptic world view. He used this admittedly unsatisfactory conceptual framework because it was the only means of communication with his contemporaries. Such a theory poses a psychological anomaly. If Jesus were a true man with a fully human mind, how could he transcend the limitations of his time? Orthodoxy had a ready answer. By virtue of the *communicatio idiomatum* the human nature shared so fully in the divine omniscience that the teachings of Jesus are free of error. Reformed theologians were willing to admit that Jesus had to learn. Riisenius said, "He was endued with knowledge great above all others, but yet finite and created, to which something could be added and truly was added."[3] But what he did teach, while finite in scope, was nonetheless true. The Pietist Zinzendorf went even farther in admitting the limitations of Jesus. As a child, Zinzendorf maintained, Jesus had to learn the Bible and with it he learned "much rabbinic rubbish." It was by the indwelling of the Holy Spirit that he forgot the errors and remembered only the truth.

The new Christology was committed to a proposition of a different order. By virtue of his genius as a moral and religious teacher, it was argued, Jesus was free of the intellectual and moral limitations of his age. Although he used the language of miracles and eschatology, he was actually living out of a consciousness that transcends such irrationalities. This assertion existed as an unexamined premise behind the new image of Christ. But could such an idea be supported by historical research? The necessity for some accommodation theory in the new Christologies was evident. But there seemed to be painfully scanty evidence in the New Testament that this was the way in which Jesus thought.

## The Fragments and What They Fragmented

Gotthold Ephraim Lessing (1729–1781), dramatist and philosopher of the Enlightenment, was given the post of librarian at the ducal library of Wolfenbüttel by the Duke of Brunswick in 1769. The Duke gave Lessing permission to publish works from the library free of censorship, providing they involved no attack on religion. After carefully testing the extent of his freedom, Lessing published seven essays, presumably anonymous, on religion. These so-called *Wolfenbüttel Fragments* were actually part of a larger work left in manuscript form by Hermann Samuel Reimarus (1694–1768), a professor of Oriental languages at Hamburg. The *Fragments* deal with a variety of topics from the viewpoint of radical deism. The most crucial for the future of Christology are "Concerning the Story of the Resurrection" and "The Intention of Jesus and His Disciples." Lessing published the *Fragments* not so much as their uncritical advocate as a polemicist anxious to use them in his own battles. He saw them as a means of combating the Biblical literalism of orthodoxy and the half-Biblical, half-philosophical theology of the neologians. He believed the *Fragments* shattered all prevailing notions about revelation in Jesus and the Bible. They called for a new alternative beyond orthodox obscurantism and neology. They called forth an extended defense of orthodoxy by Chief Pastor Johann Melchior Goeze of Hamburg and of the neologians by none other than Semler. Semler, the innovator of mid-century, became, by the end of the century, the anguished defender of his own modernism against a modernism more radical still.

Theologically, Reimarus followed in the tradition of radical English deism. In "The Impossibility of a Revelation Which All Men Should Have Good Grounds for Believing," he advanced the same argument against historical revelation as had Tindal in *Christianity as Old as Creation*. Having secured his religion on philosophical grounds, he moved on to analyze the New Testament historically. He turned to his task motivated by hatred of the distortions and perversions of human religious life which he believed spring from belief in a particular, historical revelation. He wrote with the zeal of a prosecuting attorney laying bare the contradictions and frauds of a defendant long held in high honor by his community. Unlike the neologians or thoroughgoing rationalists Reimarus felt no commitment to the preservation of Christianity. He was under no compulsion to preserve Jesus as a perfect teacher of natural religion. He felt neither the need to dignify natural religion by association with Jesus nor the need to support Jesus as a teacher of philosophical virtue. He was free to ask the crucial historical question, Just how did Jesus relate to the Jewish-apocalyptic world view of his day?

Reimarus realized that most Christian reconstructions of the life of Jesus and the apostles were lamed from the beginning by the tendency to read later doctrinal formulas back into the earliest strata of history. The key to understanding Jesus is "not out of our accepted catechism opinions, but out of places in the Old Testament and the Gospels."[4] One basic fact emerges from a fully historical approach. There is a basic distinction to be made between the teachings of Jesus and those of his disciples. The teachings of the disciples are not an interpretation of Jesus' teachings. The disciples' religion is a new religion. It is the foundation of Christianity. The religion of Jesus was Judaism. He was not founding a new religion. He taught that he had no intention of abolishing the law. Rather, he was announcing himself as the Messiah who would fulfill the expectations of the Jews. The Jews of Jesus' time were expecting the imminent coming of the Kingdom of God. It was this of which Jesus spoke when he declared, "Repent, for the kingdom of God is at hand." Theological rationalism had misunderstood the apocalyptic eschatology as the basis for Jesus' understanding of the Kingdom. The new theology had taught that Jesus was not referring to an exclusivistic eschatological Kingdom but the ever-growing community of all those committed to ethical living. Jesus brought people into this kingdom by teaching and motivating them to moral effort. Jesus had certainly never interpreted the Kingdom of God in the modern progressive moralistic fashion. In fact, Reimarus observes, Jesus did not define the Kingdom as such. He proclaimed the coming of a kingdom the meaning of which was already known to his contemporaries. This meaning is found in Judaism and the Old Testament. Jesus was preaching the coming of the Davidic kingdom promised in Moses and the prophets. This kingdom was to come through him. He was its promised Messiah. "In the first Christian church the catechism and the confession of faith were short. They need only believe the Gospel, or have trust that Jesus would soon begin the kingdom of God. If they would but manifest their readiness to repent, then they would be baptized and were perfect Christians."[5] The kingdom was to be exclusively for Jews. It was an earthly, political kingdom based on the victory of the Messiah over the enemies of the Jewish people. In his role as Messiah, Jesus can rightfully be called "the Son of God." But there was in the title no hint of a doctrine of the divinity of Christ. Understood against its Jewish background the title designates a human being appointed by God for some special high task.

Jesus' vivid awareness of the imminent coming of the kingdom of which he was Messiah led to two attempts at popular uprisings during his lifetime. The first was when he sent out his disciples on a preaching mission to "the towns of Israel" (Matt. 10:1–23). His hope that people would rally to his cause was disappointed. The second attempt was at his entry into Jerusalem. Relying on the help of his followers, he defied the authorities in the hope of a rebellion. With his failure to start an uprising the authorities seized Jesus. His mission as a political messiah had failed. Condemned to crucifixion, he dies in despair, his last words being, "My God, my God, why hast thou forsaken me?" The meaning is clear: "God had not helped him in his intention and purpose."[6] This is the end of Jesus and his messianic mission. Yet this marked not the end but only the beginning of Christianity.

The notion of a shift early in the history of the faith away from the message of Jesus to the forms of churchly Christianity was not a new one. Since the writings of the sixteenth-century radicals the idea of the perversion of the religion of Jesus into early Roman Catholicism had been a staple of the new theology. The perversion had come with the admixture of Hellenistic philosophy and the engrafting of the church into the life of the state. Reimarus pushes the perversion of Jesus' message back into the apostolic age. It was the work of the disciples themselves as they faced the failure of Jesus' political messianism. Faced with the calamitous end of their hopes, the disciples, who were to have been judges in this new kingdom, were left to return to their former ways of life. But how bleak the life of a fisherman appeared after being a herald of the kingdom. So they quickly set about the development of a new system of teaching that would allow them to keep on preaching in the name of Jesus despite his death. At this point Reimarus' offense to the sensibilities of his age reaches its apogee. The evolution of Christianity was based upon a fraud by which the disciples managed to maintain themselves in the privileged position of preachers despite the failure of the very thing they had been proclaiming. In contrast to Jesus' teaching, Christianity became a religion of spiritual, otherworldly redemption offered to all men because of the death and resurrection of a Savior figure. It called for a faith that was in reality the acceptance of speculative doctrines about the Savior.

The source of apostolic doctrine was Jewish eschatology. It was not the political messianism of Jesus but the apocalyptic eschatology going back to The Book of Daniel. In distinction to the political eschatology, the apocalyptic was based on two appearances of the Messiah, the first in lowliness, the second in glory. This was to be the key to the new system of doctrine. The apostles arranged to steal the body of Jesus and proclaim his resurrection. This formed the basis for teaching that Jesus had gone to heaven and would soon return. They could appeal back to Jesus' proclamation of the imminent coming of the Kingdom for authority. Resurrection was also the basis of their atonement doctrine in which Jesus had died for the sins of the world and was risen to show his victory over them. In the light of the promised Second Coming it was possible to continue the proclamation of the Kingdom. Yet even this proved embarrassing because the Second Coming was delayed. Eventually the Second Coming was pushed into the background and Christianity became a religion of spiritual, otherworldly salvation. The shift in doctrine made necessary a complete reshuffling of the evidence about the historical Jesus into the form it now has in the Gospels. "Thus, the new system is not determined by history, but history must be determined according to the new system."[7]

Reimarus had done an amazing piece of historical interpretation. He brought into coherent relationship the disparate traditions of New Testament thought. His schema for historical reconstruction was drawn from historical sources—Jewish eschatology—rather than from the nonhistorical dogmas of philosophical religion or Christian orthodoxy. He posed the most severe problems for the newly emerging Protestantism. He had shown that there is no historical grounds for remaking Jesus into a teacher of a rationalistic religion and prudential ethic. Jesus lived and worked within a world view foreign to modern man. His significance cannot be rescued by picturing him as a crypto-eighteenth-century man in the first century. Any future claims of revelation in Christ had to deal with the fact that revelation was enunciated within the discredited world view of Jewish eschatology. However, Reimarus remains one of those scholars who, although brilliantly correct on some questions, blunts the cutting edge of his thought by being wrong on others. He mistakenly made a radical separation between the political and apocalyptic eschatology, so that only the political could apply to Jesus and only the apocalyptic to the apostles. The two actually came together. Similarly, his thesis of conscious fraud could not explain Christian doctrine. He was blinded by his rationalistic presuppositions to the creative forces at work in early Christianity which go far beyond the limits of a conscious fraud. "The solution offered by Reimarus may be wrong; the data of observation from which he starts out are, beyond question, right, because the primary datum of all is genuinely historical."[8]

Reimarus perceived that a radically historical treatment of Christian origins called for a new approach to the problem of verification. The new theology of the eighteenth century had offered as verification of Christ's revelation either the conformity of his message with natural religion or the evidence of fulfilled prophecy and miracle. If Jesus' message is deeply caught up in Jewish eschatology, the first verification has been removed. With little further ado Reimarus sweeps aside the other verifications in order. In conclusion, Reimarus claims that the only possible verification for Christianity is an empirical fact that will support the central contention of the apostles' preaching— the Second Coming of Christ. Historical proofs have only to do with what has happened in the past. A particular miracle or prophecy can at best prove only one isolated fact. Christianity is a faith about something that will happen in the future and something universal in scope. No amount of arguing about the past can ever show with certainty what is to happen in the future. Only in that moment when future promise becomes contemporary event can the promise be verified as true or false. Lessing, Reimarus' great publicist, caught the force of his contention about the weakness of historical proofs in his essay "On the Proof of the Spirit and of Power." It is only the present reality of a religion that can prove its validity.

> Therein lies the problem that reports of fulfilled prophecies are not fulfilled prophecies; that the reports of miracles are not miracles. These, the prophecies fulfilled before my eyes, the miracles that occur before my eyes, are immediate in their effect. But those—the reports of fulfilled prophecies and miracles—have to work through a medium which takes away all their force.[9]

Since the Second Coming has not occurred, and other proofs are false and inadequate, Reimarus concludes that the Christian evaluation of Jesus is wrong. The historical prop of the new Christology has been removed. The picture of Jesus as the ethical and religious teacher maintaining in the first century the code of natural religion is not historically tenable. Verification of the truth of Jesus' religious revelation was cast in an entirely new perspective by his involvement with eschatology. The question of revelation in Christ had to be approached in a manner far beyond the scope of either Semler or Goeze. The Christology of the future was to be formed in new and uncharted territory.

## The Naturalness of Natural Religion

In back of the most radical freethinker and the most conservative neologian stood a common set of assumptions about man's knowledge of God. Common to both Reimarus and Semler was belief in the doctrines of natural religion. There were deep differences over the place of Christ in revealing these truths to mankind. But it was assumed that belief in one God, human moral obligation, freedom, and immortality were rational ideas supported by sound reasoning. Reimarus may have argued that men could know these things with certainty only through reason. Yet his most conservative opponent would never think of arguing that these doctrines were irrational ideas imparted to man in a fashion that vitiated his rational powers. Both conservative and radical had shunned one vital task. Having been critical of many things, they still had the task of examining critically the philosophical assumptions behind natural religion. Theology and philosophy had to examine its critical tool —reason—critically. Just how natural was natural religion? The Scottish historian and philosopher David Hume and a Königsberg philosopher Immanuel Kant (1724–1804) were to carry out this task.

The theoretical basis of natural religion had been somewhat variously conceived. Lord Herbert had undertaken its construction on purely deductive-rationalistic grounds. Locke had conceived it on empirical grounds. Leibniz and Wolff had seen the basis of a natural theology established in an a priori fashion by application of the law of noncontradiction. In every case the bare bones of philosophical argumentation had been given substance by reference to the picture of the universe given by the new science. The most popular starting point was the argument from design. Bishop Butler felt the argument from design was the impregnable answer to unbelief, even for those uninitiated in philosophy or physics. All that was needed was an open mind.

> There is no need of abstruse reasonings and distinctions to convince the unprejudiced understanding, that there is a God who made and governs the world, and will judge it with righteousness. . . . To an unprejudiced mind ten thousand instances of design cannot but prove a designer.[10]

Parallel to the physical order of the universe is the moral order, presided over by God the Judge who punishes the wicked and rewards the good. Just as the physical order so the moral operates according to its own laws which can be known by men through their reason. Hume raised the sharpest questions about this whole line of reasoning. Is the argument from design theoretically justified or practically relevant to the concerns of religion? The argument from design, for Hume, is basically an argument from an effect—the physical and moral order of the universe—back to a cause—God the Creator.

The validity of arguments from an effect back to a cause is limited and can never produce absolute certainty. Both these limitations make it an unsuitable argument for establishing the existence of a God universal in scope and who must be infallibly known by believers. The argument from design fails, in the first place, according to Hume, because it ascribes an infinite cause—a morally perfect and all-powerful God—to a finite effect—the order and justice we see about us in the world. The order of the world is only finite and its justice imperfect. There is no need to predicate an infinitely just and omnipotent Creator to explain these things. "When we infer any particular cause from an effect, we must proportion the one to the other, and can never be allowed to ascribe to the cause any qualities, but what are exactly sufficient to produce the effect." For as Hume concludes, "A wise man therefore proportions his belief to the evidence."[11] If belief in God is proportioned to the evidence according to Hume's prescription, such a God becomes an object of little religious significance. "An abstract, invisible object, like that which *natural* religion alone presents to us, cannot long actuate the mind, or be of any moment in life."[12] The finite God of natural religion is a far cry from the omnipotent God of traditional theism.

More crucial in the long run was Hume's critique of causality itself. The notion of causality, if utilized with due regard for the proportionality of cause to effect, is a useful idea. For all his skepticism Hume never doubted this. But do causal inferences have a necessity about them that allows us to deduce a specific cause from a given effect with certainty? Hume's answer is no. "All effects follow not with like certainty from their supposed causes." Yet this is precisely what is being assumed in the argument from design. The certainty of the existence of God comes as a necessary conclusion from the order of the universe. Legitimately the argument from an effect can suggest a possible cause, as it does in the framing of scientific hypothesis. Such a line of reasoning can always be tested by further experience. A conclusion has a potential experiential verification when made about finite things which is lacking when the conclusion is to the existence of an infinite God. The infinite God of traditional theism is "a single being . . . not comprehended under any species or genus." He is transcendent and incomprehensible. He is of a different order of reality and cannot be verified by anything less than himself.

The nerve of the argument from design is in a false conception of the necessary and inevitable interconnection of cause and effect. This is a metaphysical assumption struck down by observation. There is, according to Hume, no perception that establishes the notion of causality. Human perceptions are only of the succession of one event, the cause, followed by another event, the effect. The causal relation is inferred by men. But no perception includes the notion of a necessary and inevitable interconnection. The human tendency to absolutize the notion of causal relationships is an important means to order and clarify experience. However, this is a tendency of the human mind, not of reality itself. The notion of causality is absolutely grounded in the human mind and only provisionally in reality. When natural theology is critically revised in this light it "resolves itself into one simple, though somewhat ambiguous, at least undefined, proposition, *that the cause or causes of order in the universe probably bear some remote analogy to human intelligence.*"[13]

## Awaking from Dogmatic Slumbers

When Kant said that the reading of Hume had awakened him from his "dogmatic slumbers" he was referring not to the dogmas of a revealed religion but rather to those of a regnant philosophy. The dogmatic certainties of Wolffian rationalism were a heavy hand on German intellectual life in the eighteenth century. The assumption behind the rationalistic description of reality was simple. By the proper exercise of human intelligence men can know what is ultimately real. Hume had raised the crucial question about this assumption in Kant's mind. Kant set out on the monumental task of critically analyzing the human capacity for knowledge, judgment, and values. The outcome was an intellectual revolution. The first and most evident impact of his analysis was the completion of the critique of natural theology. Hume had reduced the God of the theistic proofs to a pale shadow of his former self. Kant reduced him still further to the status of a possible idea. Implicit in all theistic proofs is the ontological argument. Hidden behind Thomas Aquinas or Newton or Bishop Butler, Kant argues, stands Anselm with his assertion that the thought of a Supreme Being includes necessarily the actual existence of such a Being. Theistic proofs assume that establishing a convincing line of argument about God also establishes the real existence of God. The fallacy of the ontological argument is the underlying fallacy of all theistic proofs. In fact, Kant goes even farther. The fallacy of the ontological argument is the fallacy behind all rationalistic arguments about ultimate reality. Pure thought is not an unambiguous guide to reality. The results of all thinking must be checked against further experience if its validity is to be established.

Hume had driven the entering wedge with which Kant was to fell the theistic proofs. Hume taught that there is nothing logically contradictory in the nonexistence of anything. "Whatever is may not be" since "no negation of fact can involve a contradiction." "That Caesar, or the angel Gabriel, or any being never existed may be a false proposition, but still is perfectly conceivable and implies no contradiction."[14] By applying the rules of pure thought the human mind cannot decide on existence since from a logical standpoint they are both equally possible. Asserting the nonexistence of a single First Cause is not logically contradictory. It simply implies an equally logical assertion that there is no First Cause, or that there are several first causes. Kant now takes this analysis of the relation of existence to thought one step farther. Kant asks what attributing the predicate "being" does to an object of thought. His answer is simply that it does nothing. "By whatever and by whatever number of predicates—even to the complete determination of it—I may cogitate a thing I do not in the least augment the object of my conception by the addition of the statement, this thing exists."[15] The ontological argument is a kind of word trick men play on themselves. From the standpoint of pure thought there is only one thing that can be said about the word "is": it is a connective between subject and predicate. The question of actual existence is a question of a different order. The existence of an object or being cannot be determined by thought alone but is dependent on experience. Here was an assertion of revolutionary import for theology. Men do not establish the existence of God on theoretical grounds and then experience him. Rather, men know of God's existence because of their experience of him. The gateway to theology is not through rationality but through experience.

There remained for Kant a puzzle posed by the history of philosophy. Why had so many able philosophers in times past concluded for the existence of God on the basis of the argument from design? The objections to the argument seem self-evident to Kant. Why had the problems not been more self-evident to others? Obviously the force of tradition has been strong. But there is a still deeper reason that the argument from design has been so prevalent. This is the nature of human reason itself. "Human reason is by nature architectonic." Reason seeks to structure and unify experience. "The architectonic interest of reason requires a unity, not empirical, but *a priori* and rational."[16] The mistake of the precritical—that is to say, pre-Kantian—philosopher was to convert this tendency of reason into a doctrine about a perfect unitary Being existing apart from the world. Instead, Kant said, the rational structure of experience comes from the mind and in itself does not decide whether there is such a Supreme Being. Critical philosophy exposes the limits of reason. Reason can legitimately exercise its unifying function on experience. But men are misled if they believe that pure reason can give knowledge of a realm beyond experience. Reason is not the universal solvent of man's deepest questions. Within its proper sphere reason is sovereign. It is man's capacity to work and think creatively about experience. It is not a link to some unseen world. It is our guide to this world. Once reason passes beyond its sphere from the phenomenal to the noumenal world, it can be betrayed into antinomies. At best,

Kant said, reason can show us the structure of a possible idea of God.

The Kantian critique extended also to the other doctrines of natural religion—freedom and immortality. Just as in the doctrine of God, here also reason is unable to avoid contradiction. The certainty of these doctrines must be established in a realm other than pure reason. The effects of this critical philosophy on the modernization of Christology were profound. It had been certainty about the doctrines of natural religion that had made possible doubt about orthodoxy. But if human reason is unable to supply men with certainty in religion, what shall? No longer was it a question of whether one was willing to go all the way with Reimarus in rejecting revelation on the basis of reason or only to the halfway house of Semler. A corner had been turned. What now was to provide intellectual basis for building a modern expression of the Christian faith?

*Chapter IX*

# THE END

# AND THE BEGINNING

## Reason and Reaction

The mind of David Hume on religious questions is often hidden behind "the successive wrappings of discretion." In two contrasting passages at the end of his *Dialogues Concerning Natural Religion,* he gives striking expression to the reactions of his contemporaries to the meaning of critical philosophy for the future of religion. In the first passage, Hume is revealing himself. He reflects on the plight of a man "inquisitive, contemplative and religious." Before the question of God and "of a particular providence and of a future state," where is such a man left?

> Some astonishment, indeed, will naturally arise from the greatness of the object, some melancholy from its obscurity, some contempt of human reason that it can give no solution more satisfactory with regard to so extraordinary and magnificent a question.[1]

The man who looks at the "religious hypothesis" critically can conclude only that it is "not capable of extension, variation or more particular explication, . . . and it affords no inference that affects human life." Despite his hunger for more, man must live in the light of what he can really know. We need not fear

151

this state of affairs. Contrary to what is usually believed, "the ties of morality" will not be loosened, nor is the demise of the religious hypothesis "pernicious to the peace of civil society." The wise magistrate can still deal justly. The good man can still live wisely. The principles of the great modern religious systems have fostered intolerance, subverted sincerity and self-knowledge. Man may now be free of this curse. Secular man had made his debut. Critical historical reflections had separated him from dogma and special revelation. Now critical philosophy separated him from a knowledge of God. This liberation which Hume announced with wistfulness and irony was being celebrated with strident glee by his French contemporaries. The age of religion is at an end. "The intemperance of the mind," against which Bishop Bossuet had warned at the beginning of the century was now running its course. "A grand assault upon the Church" was under way. Modern thought had won its victory over Christ. For many this was to be the final word on the modernization of Christianity. It had been tried and had failed. In the wonderland of modern philosophy, God, like the Cheshire Cat in Alice's Wonderland, was fading away, leaving only a smile. Or perhaps in the light of Hume's early Calvinistic upbringing, it would be more accurate to say he disappeared, leaving only a frown. Jesus may be retained as a teacher and martyr or scorned as a knave and fraud. In the final measure of things, this was a matter of indifference to a world come of age. The crucial matter was that modern men need no longer confess that "God was in Christ reconciling the world unto himself," but can be busy remaking this world.

A second passage in the conclusion of the *Dialogues* revealed another spirit at work in Hume's age. In all likelihood, Hume made these statements in a thin concealment of his contempt. Yet, nonetheless, he gauged accurately the reaction of many of his contemporaries to the critique of natural theology.

> A person, seasoned with a just sense of the imperfections of natural religion, will fly to revealed truth with the greatest avidity. . . . To be a philosophical sceptic is, in a man of letters, the first and most essential step toward a sound, believing Christian.[2]

The critique of natural theology opened the way for a new religious conservatism. It was destined during the nineteenth century to be a tremendous force on the institutional and intellectual life of Christendom. It is a voice still to be heard. The new conservatism was shaped by a host of forces—intellectual, religious, social, and political. At its center stands the intellectual transition Hume described. Philosophical skepticism can become the key to theological dogmatism. If human reason cannot pronounce on the transcendent, then revelation can. Critical philosophy clears the way for revelation by pointing out to men the limitation of their intellects. Within a few years of its writing, Kant's *Critique of Pure Reason* was seized upon by Prof. Gottlob Christian Storr (1746–1805) and his followers in the "old Tübingen School" as a weapon against theological rationalism. The conservatives abominated Kant's religious and ethical ideas. But his analysis of reason and its limitations became a staple item in their polemic arsenal. The limitations of man's reason which Christian faith had long acknowledged in its doctrine of original sin now found support in the critical school of philosophy. Dismayed by the creeping hegemony of rationalism, the new conservatives took a positive delight in the incapacity of the human mind. The result was a romantic attachment to authoritarian anti-intellectualism.

This new conservatism gave the traditional Christology renewed vitality. Philosophical and moral arguments advanced since the sixteenth century against the conventions of orthodoxy were swept aside. Men must be prepared to recognize the inevitable clash between the truths of revelation and the arrogance of the ungodly mind. Leading architect of the new conservatism in Germany, Ernst Wilhelm Hengstenberg (1802–1869), professor of theology in Berlin, gave eloquent expression to this belief. "Not every irrationality is a Christian dogma, but every Christian dogma is unreasonable, not in itself, but to our reason which has become unreasonable through the fall."[3] Natural theology is, for him, only able to find an idol, not the true God. Rationalism was simply arrogant unbelief. Hengstenberg recapitulated in his own life the logic of the new conservatism. He started his academic career as a rationalist, writing for his doctoral dissertation a purely philological study of the Old Testament in the spirit of the current critical opinion. He experienced a deeply felt conversion through his contact with a pietistic group of students that led him to reject rationalistic versions of Christianity for a newfound orthodoxy. He pledged himself, after his "rebirth" to teach only out of "the obedience of faith"—long a darling term of the movement—and wrote for his licensure thesis an exegesis of Isa., ch. 53, as a messianic prophecy. He had forsaken the unbelief of the higher critics and went on to produce his major work, *Christology of the Old Testament*. Using every technique of allegory and typology, he went far beyond Locke or the deists in their concern for messianic prophecies in the Old Testament. His *Christology of the Old Testament* was a massive apologetic work against historical exegesis. "Christ," he maintained, "was the central point of the whole of the Old Testament."[4] To argue against this point was only possible for those who had "lost their capacity for an impartial examination of prophecy and history through their ungodliness of mind."[5] The rejection of the apologetic from miracle and fulfilled prophecy was, at worst, human arrogance, at best, the result of a blindness of mind and coldness of heart engendered by rationalism. In a typically romantic criticism of rationalism, Hengstenberg attributes Grotius' historical, critical exegesis to "his cold, prosaic mind which unfitted him for comprehending such intuitions as far transcend the limits of ordinary experience."[6]

The forces that rendered the rebirth of traditional Christology possible were not simply intellectual. It was the whole tenor of the times. The French Revolution had forced upon Europe a reappraisal of the intellectual developments which championed reason and the rights of man. This reappraisal was a negative one. All of a sudden, the descendants of those crotchety parsons who had forced Frederick I to unseat Professor Wolff because of his subversive rationalism had a powerful new argument. The French Revolution proved to them in a frightening way that what their forefathers had been saying was correct. No compromise is allowed in the alliance of absolutist religion with an absolutist state. The reaction from the revolution provided a basis for returning to the old policies for state and church. The new conservatives of the restoration time in France exulted uncritically in authoritarianism. Only as an infallible church is linked with an absolutist state can society be rebuilt after being wrecked on the principles of 1789—liberty, equality, fraternity. In Protestant lands the alliance between religious and political conservatism, while less flamboyant than that in France, was nonetheless at work. Hengstenberg and his followers allied themselves with the political conservatism and nationalism in Berlin. Hengstenberg wanted to unite his party's religious conservatism with that of the emerging German state to ensure a hand in vital church and university appointments. This alliance of political and religious conservatism was the result of a deep and abiding fear. Yet one fact remains: for many the new conservatism helped to vivify a theology other men had declared long since dead. The devotees of theological enlightenment had underestimated the irrational forces that were to shape the beliefs of modern men.

Coupled with the intellectual and political forces behind the conservative theology of the postcritical age was a series of religious movements that touched the spiritual life of modern Christendom. From the end of the eighteenth century, movements of spiritual renewal were energizing popular religion in Europe, England, and America. The reaction of the church to modernity was not simply intellectual but also institutional reorganization. The intellectual objections to traditional religious dogmas were after all a problem for only a minority. This minority wrote the books by which we study the past, yet their problems and accomplishments touched only a few. The most ominous problem of Christendom was finding religious forms that could communicate a vital faith to the majority whose lives were also being changed by the history of the time. The great state churches that dominated European religious life were becoming increasingly ineffective. The new urban dwellers created by the industrial revolution were alienated from traditional churches. The peasants and small-town tradesmen were often numbed by a theological rationalism they could not understand, or an officially delivered orthodoxy they could not experience. Into this situation came the modern movement of revival: Methodist and Calvinistic revivals in England and America and revitalized Pietism in Germany. These revival movements had in common an individualistic Christocentric piety. They presented the person and work of Christ not as a doctrine to be contemplated intellectually but as an experience. This revivalism focused on the turning point of conversion through a personal experience of Christ. Conversion was founded not on rational assent but on a dramatic turn of the will. By its success in communicating the Christian experience of forgiveness and new life, revivalism deflected attention from its intellectual shortcomings. In revivalism, Christological orthodoxy found its most powerful argument against modernity.

In the seventeenth century, Pietism and orthodoxy had stood in opposition. By the end of the eighteenth century, Pietism and orthodoxy had fused. The pietistic experience of new birth becomes the motive power that allows men to accept the orthodoxy of the church. In the English-speaking world the elements of formal orthodoxy in the theology of the revivalistic groups were minimal. It was, by and large, a truncated Calvinism or Arminianism that, despite differences on predestination, preserved Christological orthodoxy. In Germany, Pietism became the gateway for reestablishing the whole of Lutheran orthodoxy. The thinking of the new conservatives moved in a tightly knit circle. To believe in revelation, they argued, is to believe in the Bible. To believe in the Bible is to believe in the dogmas of churchly orthodoxy.

From the end of the eighteenth century, with the rise of the critical and conservative theologies, the relation of the intellectual to the institutional life of the church became increasingly complex. There had been a fluctuation of alienation and return since the beginnings of the modernization of theology. The first modern Christologies were the work of outsiders. By the end of the seventeenth century in England, churchmen still had little part in the new development which even to the more open-minded seemed tinged with heresy. Locke and the deists were philosophers, scientists, historians, or men of affairs. By the middle of the eighteenth century in Germany, the modernizing trends were accepted into the life of the church for consideration, if not full-scale adoption. Semler and the neologians all held professorial chairs in theology or major church posts. With the new radicalism in history and philosophy—Reimarus, Hume, and Kant—the tide of reaction set in. A new religious conservatism swept along by the tides of revival and undergirded by Restoration political fervor, set loose a wave of alienation. Storr in Tübingen and Hengstenberg and his party in Berlin had enough power within the institutional life of the church to keep alive a repressive dogmatic system well into the nineteenth century. Strauss lost his post as "repetent" at Tübingen and was later barred from a professorship in Zurich. Kant haggled with censors and finally had to promise Frederick William II he would be silent on religious questions. Late in his career the neologian Spalding retired from public life in protest. The power of the new conservatism was not absolute. Great figures, like Schleiermacher, became leaders deeply related to church life, despite a hefty conservative resistance. By 1826 Ferdinand Christian Baur was appointed a professor at Tübingen. Reaction or renewal in church life often became a matter of personalities varying with the interplay of power groups in church and government. One thing was clear. Semler's great dream of an intellectually renewed church leading a spiritually renewed nation was not to be fulfilled. Instead of the intellectual and spiritual life of Christendom being clarified, it entered a period of ambiguity within which it lives to this day. It is symbolic that the next chapter in Christology was written by a philosopher, and one alienated from the church at that.

## Christ Within the Limits of Reason Alone

Kant was a critic but also a builder. As critic he sealed the doom of the old rationalistic natural religion and with it a whole era of Christology. As a builder he provided foundations for a new era. His foundations proved broader than the building he reared. His Christology is transitional. It shares the world of his contemporaries, while it intimates the shape of the future. The inner complexity in his Christology springs from something

deeper than the usual turgidity of Kantian prose. In his religious
and ethical writings two different Christologies are intertwined.
Kant believed he had reconciled the two. But in modern theology
the two became separated. On one level, Kant can be read as
providing a new basis for continuing the reinterpretation of
Christology in the light of natural religion. Jesus emerges as
the great ethical-religious teacher and example. In this respect
C. C. J. Webb is correct in saying, " 'Natural religion' or, to use
Kant's own phrase, 'religion within the limits of mere reason'
finds its last great exponent in the philosopher of Königsberg."[7]
The difference between Kant and his predecessors is his grounding natural religion in ethics rather than in metaphysics. Kant
made the crucial connection between metaphysical skepticism
and ethical positivism which played a major role in the liberal
Protestantism of Ritschl and Harnack. The Kantian ethical
reformulation of religion with Jesus as its great interpreter became the cornerstone on which nineteenth-century liberalism
was built. Like its predecessors among the Socinians, deists, and
Unitarians, this new liberalism was reductionist in its approach
to traditional dogma and Biblical materials. It sought "the essence of Christianity" in verifiable truth.

On another level, Kant provided the basis for the romantic-
idealistic reinterpretation of the nineteenth century. He was
opening the way to the theological modernism of Hegel and
Biedermann and Tillich. Kant saw in Christological orthodoxy
great truths which had to be rescued from the inept and misleading expression given them. The critique of dogma opened the
way for seeing it in a new light as symbols of the relation of God
and man. Unlike the Ritschlian liberalism, modernism is not
reductionist. Modernism seeks not some core of truth from
amid irrationality; rather, by reinterpretation it translates the
truth, ineptly expressed, in the teachings of the past. The key to
modernism is not reduction but reinterpretation. Christological
doctrine is not the quasi-historical, quasi-metaphysical account
of the origins of Jesus. Yet it is not for this reason rejected. The
truth to which these doctrines witness is recaptured in the light
of a faith rooted in morality. As Kant himself put it: "Ecclesiastical faith [dogmatic orthodoxy] has pure religious faith
[faith rooted in morality] as its highest interpreter."[8]

In a postcritical age the religious hypothesis is not to be established by theoretical reason. The true entrée is through moral experience. The starting point is the basic human experience of "oughtness," the obligation to follow the moral law. This experience of oughtness is an unqualified, or to use Kant's term, "a categorical imperative." The ethical imperative is not justified by its place in some grand metaphysical plan or by a system of rewards and punishments. Man does not first solve the metaphysical problem of freedom and determinism and then conclude the correctness of moral obligation. The moral imperative is a direct, immediate intuition. Men may pervert or disregard it, but from it they never escape. The primary implication of the categorical imperative is belief in human freedom. The moral imperative is not a mockery of man. The very fact that men have respect for the moral law implies they have the freedom to fulfill it. Kant hoped to extricate himself from the metaphysical problem of human freedom that plagued the interpreters of the scientific world view. Moralists were confounded in explaining how man could be free in the deterministic world described by science. Critical philosophy is of crucial importance at this point. By showing that the causal determinism of science is not necessarily the structure of ultimate reality, Kant opened the way to his moral teachings. There is an experience, he argues, as real and valid as that of our empirical intuitions of the world. This is the experience of moral obligation and freedom. This freedom is "one which is not determinable by physical laws, and consequently is not capable of empirical intuition in proof of its reality, but, nevertheless, completely justifies its objective reality *a priori* in the pure practical law."[9]

Immediately linked with freedom as a necessary moral belief is the notion of the highest good, *summum bonum*. Again Kant touches a problem prominent among theologians and ethicists of the seventeenth and eighteenth centuries. Does man pursue moral goodness for its own sake or for hope of reward? Kant refuses to separate these ideas as mutually exclusive alternatives. Instead, he brings them together in his notion of the *summum bonum*. Whereas moral duty must be fulfilled for its own sake and not for any reward, the ideal situation is one in which virtue and happiness exist together. This is the *summum bonum*. To believe in it is to believe in the ultimate justice of the universe. The coincidence of moral obedience and happiness is the ultimate fulfillment of man. Kant was not unaware of the paradox of Job—the sufferings of the righteous in this world. "We cannot expect in this world by the most punctilious observance of the moral laws any necessary connection of happiness and virtue adequate to the *Summum Bonum*."[10] If men had only the evidence of this world, they could well take the moral law to be a false guide. Such a loss of moral faith would be the greatest calamity. Faith in the *summum bonum* is not an irrational will-o'-the-wisp. The basis for the attainment of the *summum bonum* becomes intelligible only in the light of the existence of God as the guarantor of the ultimate coordination of virtue and happiness. He is the ground of a future life in which men know perfect virtue and justice.

Three postulates are implicit in the moral imperative which makes it intelligible: freedom, immortality, and God. These three postulates are not "theoretical dogmas" of either religion or reason. They are postulates implicit in the experience of the moral imperative as the ground of its possibility. Although they are revealed by a chain of reasoning, their explication is not a proof based on theoretical reason. It is the analysis of something given directly in moral experience. The being of God in himself, the metaphysical grounds of human freedom and immortality, still remain a mystery to us. The scope of our theoretical knowledge is not enlarged by the postulates of practical reason. Certainty about the postulates is "in the practical point of view." This certainty comes through the active reshaping of life by the moral law. God, freedom, and immortality, Kant concludes, are "the possibility of which no human intelligence will ever fathom, but the truth of which, on the other hand, no sophistry will ever wrest from the conviction of the commonest man."[11]

> Morality thus leads ineluctably to religion, through which it extends itself to the idea of a powerful moral Lawgiver, outside of mankind, for whose will that is the final end (of creation) which at the same time can and ought to be man's final end.[12]

In its basic teachings, not in its philosophical foundations, the rational religion of Kant is the old natural religion of the deists and neologians. God, freedom, and immortality are simply the doctrines of natural religion founded in a new way. In this perspective Kant is the eighteenth century's last and most thoroughgoing devotee of the rationalization of Christianity into a philosophical religion of moral accomplishment. Jesus is the "Teacher of the Gospel," by whose teachings and example men are first led to a moral religion. His rejection of temptation to worldly power and glory, his willing acceptance of suffering and death, the moral purity of his teachings, all declare him to be Christ in whose discipleship a mankind acceptable to God is formed. Jesus was unique among the great moral teachers of the world. He was "the founder of the first true church." He established in history the religious community through which men became conscious of the true moral faith. The church has not been perfect. Kant excoriates the church for its lapse into *Pfaffertum*—dominance by a superstitious clergy. Yet the church has been the means by which men became aware that "religion is the recognition of all duties as divine commands." Jesus, as no other ethical teacher, taught men to obey moral duty for its own sake, not for hope of heaven or fear of hell. This created a revolution in faith and doctrine. Christianity was not simply the continuation of Judaism but the introduction of a new principle of religiosity. Jesus' revelation of the ideal of pure, uncoerced moral obedience gradually brought men to a higher and fuller recognition of God and his will. The shift in religion from ceremonialism and priestcraft to pure morality started by Jesus is reaching in the age of Enlightenment its fullest embodiment.

> And this, because, if the seed of the true religious faith, as it is now being publicly sown in Christendom, though only by a few, is allowed more and more to grow unhindered, we may look for a continuous approximation to that church, eternally uniting all men, which constitutes the visible representation of an invisible kingdom of God on earth.[13]

Kant has freed his natural-religion Christology from the encumbrance of the old arguments from prophecy and miracle.

They are a form of "moral unbelief." A moral religion is verified by its congruity with the conscience of man, not by external
events. Gone also is the necessity for maintaining that the moral
religion is historically the religion of the Bible. Morality is not
to be expounded according to the Bible; rather, "the Bible
should be expounded according to morality." Kant freely admits
that "frequently this interpretation may in the light of the text
appear forced, it may often really be forced."[14] Morality is the
interpretative principle which allows Kant to move with sovereign freedom over the historical traditions and doctrines of Biblical religion. *Religion Within the Limits of Reason Alone* gave
thoroughgoing rationalism in Christology a new lease on life.
No longer is it to be undermined by the philosophical inadequacies of the old natural-religion doctrine of Leibniz and Wolff.
Kant had not succumbed to the historical radicalism of Reimarus. Jesus has a positive role to play in the unfolding of the
moral ideal. There was the possibility here of an affirmative,
if limited, doctrine of Christ. This Christology could lay claim to
rational acceptance because it had excluded the rationally offensive idea of historical particularity in revelation in the interest
of ethical universalism.

## The Way to Modernism

To view Kant's Christology purely as an advanced species of
Enlightenment theologizing is to overlook the deepest stratum
of his religious thought. Kant has been a student of human nature too long to believe that the simple exhibition of a high
moral example could bring about the moral change mankind
needs. He did not share the optimism of his contemporaries
about human nature. Man is dominated by a radical evil. It is
not simply a failure to obey the moral law. It is man's corruption of the moral ideals themselves. "This evil is radical, because
it corrupts the grounds of all maxims [the deepest sources of
human motivation]; it is, moreover, as a natural propensity, in-
extricable by human powers."[15] This evil is not cured by moral
information, no matter how sublime. What is needed is a revolution in motivation. The change must come in the wellspring of
action or, as Kant calls it, "the ground of man's maxims." A

man can choose "by a single unchangeable decision" the good principle as the basis of his actions. "He can become a new man only by a kind of rebirth, as it were a new creation, and a change of heart." This rebirth does not make man morally perfect in an instant. Still he is upon the road of endless progress to holiness.[16]

Theology is the interpretation of the "victory of the good over the evil principle." The grounds of moral rebirth are illumined by the Bible and the great Christological doctrines of the church. Moral interpretation starts with the frank recognition of the mythological character of Biblical religion.

> Holy Scripture sets forth this intelligible moral relationship in the form of a narrative, in which two principles in man, as opposed to one another as is heaven and hell, are represented as persons outside him; who, not only put their strength against each other but also seek (the one as man's accuser, the other as his advocate) to establish their claims legally as though before a supreme judge.[17]

The Christ figure has a dual identity. Historically the Christ is Jesus of Nazareth. But as Christ he is more than Jesus the teacher. He is the Son of God, the "archetype of humanity reared and beloved by God." Christ is the symbol of the power of goodness at work in human life. This second identification of the Christ figure opens the way to all the doctrines of Trinity, incarnation, and atonement as symbolic accounts of how the moral principle transforms human life. Kant transmutes the traditional language about the preexistence of the Logos into an account of the origin of moral goodness. Goodness is God's gift to mankind. The moral archetype proceeds from God's own being, "hence he is no created thing but his only begotten Son." "The Son of God" or "archetype of humanity well-pleasing to God" is the second Person of the Trinity.

> In God we can revere the loving One—the Father; in him also, so far as he reveals himself in his all-inclusive idea, the archetype of humanity reared and beloved by him, we can revere his Son; and finally, so far as he . . . reveals love as based upon wisdom, we can revere the Holy Spirit.[18]

Traditionally the second Person is the creator and preserver of order in the world. In a world that understands its physical order scientifically, the second Person becomes the moral "Preserver of the human race, its benevolent Ruler and moral Guardian." The metaphysical becomes the moral. The immanence of the second Person of the Trinity in the world becomes the immanence of the moral principle in man. But Kant is quick to add, lest anyone be tempted to carry this interpretation to a doggedly literal conclusion, that God should not be invoked as "a multiform personality."

The entrance of the moral archetype into man is incarnation. The moral principle comes as a "descent from heaven." The moral archetype "assumed our humanity." This union is the "humiliation of the Son of God"—a kenosis—through which the Son makes himself the sharer in the sufferings and death of sinful mankind. Kant even considers the virgin birth for a possible place in the mythology of the moral archetype. He finally concludes it has no place in his Christology because its moral meaning is ambiguous at best.

The mythological language of preexistence and incarnation reveals the basic features of the moral archetype. To say the archetype is "no created thing" but "God's only begotten Son" means it is not a product of human thought or imagination. Its source is not social conditioning or philosophical speculation. When man experiences the moral imperative, he is not encountering himself, but a power that lies outside human resources. To encounter the moral archetype is to know God. To confess the incarnation is to celebrate the breakthrough of a redemption man cannot bring about himself.

> It is less possible to conceive how man, by nature evil, should of himself lay aside evil and raise himself to the ideal of holiness, than that the latter should descend to man and assume a humanity which is, in itself, not evil.[19]

The translation of traditional Christological doctrine into the moral ideal creates a new question. What is the relation of the historical Jesus to the archetype Christ? Linking the moral archetype exclusively to the historical Jesus is the popular understanding. But when moral archetype is "divested of its mystical veil, it is easy to see that, for practical purposes, its spirit and rational means have been valid and binding for the whole world and for all time." The principle of the good was not created by one man at one time.

> We need, therefore, no empirical example to make the idea of a person morally well-pleasing to God our archetype; this idea as an archetype is already present in our reason.[20]

Kant pushes the matter a step farther to insist that it is reason which imparts to Jesus his archetypal quality, not the other way around. The function of the historical Jesus is to bring pure ethical religion into a creative relation with ecclesiastical religion for its purification.

> In the appearance of the God-man, it is not that in him which strikes the senses and can be known through experience, but rather the archetype, lying in our reason, that we attribute to him, which is really the object of saving faith.[21]

Initially the split between the historical Jesus and the archetypal Christ had certain advantages. It allowed a new freedom for a thoroughly historical investigation of Jesus. Reimarus' gibe about "doctrine determining history" was turned aside. The appearance of Jesus is a fact in the phenomenal world known by sense experience. This fact is to be investigated with complete openness, using the techniques of scientific investigation. The Christ as the principle of the good is a reality in the noumenal world known by practical reason. Again there was a new openness at this point for a creative unfolding of the meaning of the Christological mythology in Bible and churchly doctrine. If theology develops by its own logic, rather than as a witness to historical revelation, it need not stand in unity with the historical Jesus. As the advancement of New Testament scholarship made clear, the relation of the Jesus of history to the Christ of faith became increasingly problematic.

## Reason, Morality, and Atonement

Atonement and justification are woven together in a complex pattern of tradition and innovation by Kant. His doctrine of radical evil and human impotence shows him heir to Lutheran orthodoxy. His rejection of substitutionary atonement shows him a man of the Enlightenment. Reconciliation is not the result of the divine indulgence. Satisfaction must be made to God for man's sin. The satisfaction cannot come from the death of Christ. Like all the Enlightenment theologians Kant believed man had to deal with his own sin. Satisfaction must come, by a circuitous route, from the sinner himself. Jesus' death, as a historical event, is an example of adherence to the good in the face of suffering and death. It reveals the liberty of the man who is willing to base everything on the good rather than be coerced by the powers of this world. The death of Jesus does not answer the question, How can man discharge his moral responsibility for his sins? Left to himself man is powerless. The radical evil in man brings with it "endless violations of the law and so infinite guilt." When a man chooses the good, the inevitable movement toward infinite guilt is stopped. Man is set upon a new pathway of life. Full realization of the good is not complete in this life. Yet a man is accepted by God the moment he chooses the good. God, who is free from the limitation of time, sees the moral perfection that will inevitably result from a life turned toward the good. Man is accepted now on the basis of what he will become. This is the meaning of justification. While yet a sinner, man is fully accepted by God. Just as in orthodoxy, justification is instantaneous, but sanctification is gradual. The great divide that separates Kant from orthodoxy is that the merits which justify are not those of Christ, but of man himself.

Justification is only part of reconciliation. The other is atonement. Kant is willing to join with the traditional doctrine in the belief that "satisfaction must be rendered to Supreme Justice" for all sins. The Anselmian "satisfaction theory" claims man must either make satisfaction for his sins or suffer the consequences of them. For Kant satisfaction or suffering is not the real alternative. There is no possibility of escaping the consequences of sin, although it is necessary to add quickly that Kant did not see the punishment of sin as reaching to such dire consequences as did Anselm. Kant relates the punishment for sin to the sufferings of this life. Man receives punishment for his sins before he experiences moral rebirth. There sufferings are simply the outworking of divine justice. Men are being punished for their past sins. But the sin is still greater than the suffering. After rebirth no punishment is due because man is then well-pleasing to God. Yet, in point of fact, men do suffer punishment even after moral rebirth. The rebirth itself is suffering. "The coming forth from the corrupted into the good disposition is, in itself (as 'death of the old man,' 'the crucifying of the flesh'), a sacrifice and an entrance upon a long train of life's ills."[22] After rebirth man is on a collision course with the powers of this world. Moral obedience brings with it undeserved suffering. But it is not meaningless suffering. It serves as repayment for the sins of the past.

The sufferings of the moral man, or to use the Biblical term "the new man," are the key to a moral doctrine of substitutionary atonement. Kant reinterprets this doctrine morally by drawing a sharp distinction between "the new man," the man who has made the good principle his own, and "the old man," the man still under the power of radical evil. Although physically they are the same, morally existence as old man and new man is so distinct that sufferings of the new man are sufferings borne vicariously for another person—the old man. The good principle, which can be personified as the Son of God, now incarnate in man, bears as a vicarious substitute the suffering and death of the old man.

> And this moral disposition, the good principle, which in all its purity (like unto the purity of the Son of God) man has made his own—or, (if we personify this idea) this Son of God, himself, bears as vicarious substitute the guilt of sin for him, and indeed for all who believe in him, as savior he renders satisfaction to supreme justice by his sufferings and death.[23]

By demythologizing, Kant changed atonement from an otherworldly drama of an interchange between the Father and the Son to the human drama of struggle between the old man and the new man. The otherworldly had become this-worldly; the objective had been rendered subjective. Christology is not simply the story of one man but of man himself. When Christology becomes the mythological account of human spirituality it can be coordinated with the philosophical analysis of these same concerns. In this lies modernism's answer to the scandal of historical particularity.

In this Christology, Kant opened the way for an enrichment and expansion of the scope of Christian doctrine in the modern world. He established a possibility he realized only imperfectly. His Christology remained fragmentary. Many vital matters found no place in it. Resurrection and eschatology play no part. He is only able to salvage the doctrine of atonement by means of a forced reinterpretation. These limitations spring from an unresolved ambiguity in Kant's most basic category for religious understanding, morality. Taken in its broadest sense, morality embraces the whole actional side of human being. Morality is the account of how men relate to one another and finally to God. The moral is the realm of practical reason. It is rooted in man's power to transcend his space-time world and touch the real. In this broad sense the possibilities for doctrinal reinterpretation are almost limitless. Christian doctrine can bear its witness to the ultimate questions of human existence. Yet for Kant, morality had a more limiting definition also. Morality means in this limited sense the principles of right and wrong behavior. Morality in this perspective is finally legalism. The elements of grace and personal relationship are lost. The I–Thou of faith becomes the I–It of legalism. The realm of the moral is robbed of its dimension of depth. As Schleiermacher was to protest in his analysis of religious experience, there are dimensions of human spirituality that cannot be reduced to theoretical knowledge or ethical norms. Kant's understanding of the moral was more profound and psychologically perceptive than that of the earlier eighteenth-century rationalists whose ethical theory was dominated by the prudential search for human happiness. But it was only as the romantic philosophers and poets probed more deeply the nature of human spirituality that a broad-enough base could be found for the full-orbed Christological modernism of the nineteenth century. Kant had opened a way into the future. Others had to widen it before the Lord could pass through.

# EPILOGUE

Isaac Dorner, mediating theologian and historian of the last century, passed judgment on the Christologies of the early modern period in his *Developmental History of the Doctrine of the Person of Christ*. His judgment was affirmative, if not uncritical. He understood the religious, scientific, and philosophical movements of the early modern period as part of the unfolding history of human spirituality. In this grand panorama he saw the negative forces of modern man's alienation from Christianity and his lapse into lopsided, arid intellectualism. But these were not the final word. In modern times, man was uncovering in his philosophy and poetry a new, deeper understanding of human personality. Thought was being liberated from the abstract nonmoral categories of ancient metaphysics and finding a richer, fuller vision of God and man. This new vision led men to clearer knowledge of what God had done in Jesus Christ. Dorner saw unfolding an ever-clearer understanding of the "holy love of God" revealed in Christ. Modern philosophy, in a way at times unknown to itself, was moving humanity closer to this goal.

Dorner's estimate has gone starkly out of style. In its place has come one shaped by the theology of Karl Barth. Criticism of modern religious thought is rooted in his rejection of "natural theology." This rejection is more than a repudiation of the natural religion of the early modern period. It is the rejection of any supposed knowledge of God, except through revelation. Barth asserts in a distinctively modern and more academically sophisticated fashion what Francis Cheynell had argued in the seventeenth century. To build theology on an amalgam of truths of reason with those of revelation is to embark on a venture whose outcome is already given in its start—the replacement of revelation by reason. No matter how deep the reverence for Scripture, Christ, or divine revelation, when the criterion for revelation is its conformity with reason, revelation has, in principle, been abandoned.

The logic of such an assessment is clear but one-sided. The Barthian critique rightfully exposed the unexamined presupposition behind the early modern Christologies—the assumption of direct, positive continuity between revelation and reason. The early modern theologies were unequipped to deal with the complex dialectic of revelation and reason. Despite this limitation, the birth of modernity freed theology from the tyranny of an unexamined past. The critical work from Servetus to Kant opened the way to a fresh understanding of revelation in history. Christianity was no longer limited to a shrill reassertion of its dogmatic positions against the spiritual and intellectual challenges thrust upon it by modern life. Rather, as Troeltsch said, it became possible "to overcome history by history." As historical and rational analysis uncover the contingent, human setting out of which all particular formulations of Christianity arose, their truth could be reexpressed in terms relevant to the emerging present. This freedom is not only at work in Protestant modernism but is also basic to the so-called "neo-orthodox" theologies. Since Vatican II, it has been dramatically evident in Catholic theology. This legacy of the early modern theology is liberalism, not as a particular brand of nineteenth-century theology, but as the commitment of theology to freedom. It is the freedom to apprehend and restate Christian witness in relation to the present instead of in subservience to the past.

To appreciate the new forces loosed in this period does not obscure the problems they created. The freedom for which the early liberal theologians struggled has become for many of their heirs a burden to be escaped. The perception of development and relativity in Scripture and dogma was first possible because men believed there was one point at which they stood free of the relativities of history. By the end of the eighteenth century this assumption had been undermined. Philosophical radicalism had undermined the rationality of natural religion. Historical radicalism had undermined the rationality of Biblical religion. The way into the future was unclear. For some, it meant return to an illiberal dogmatism. For others, it marked the end of religion for modern man. In this sense, the God of Western Christendom died at the end of the eighteenth century, although it took many of his undertakers a long while to discover this. The theology of the nineteenth century found another way. It undertook a fresh analysis of man and his capacity to be addressed by God. It sought in moral response, in religious feeling, or in the dynamic unfolding of spirit some point in human experience through which man touches the reality of God. The theologies of the nineteenth century had a richness and inclusiveness unknown to the rationalism of the eighteenth. However, despite its variety and increased historical sophistication, the nineteenth century built on an assumption inherited from the earliest modernizers of theology. Man is a religious being. He has some capacity for being addressed by God which gives him a perspective for re-interpreting the religious traditions of his past.

In our own day Christian theology is being addressed by new questions more radical than those of the past. We stand in a situation not unlike that of the late eighteenth century. The intellectual schema within which we have evolved our theology are being called deeply into question by forces from without and from within the faith. We stand in clear consciousness of living in the world of religionless man. Is it possible to find some new schema for interpreting religious traditions? Or has "modern theology" finally come to an end? The future of Christian theology lies in the answers to these questions.

# NOTES

## Chapter I. THE POINT OF BEGINNING

1. Heinrich Bullinger, *Compendium Christianae Religionis decem libris comprehensum* (Tiguri, 1559), II. 2. In the citations to the Reformed and Lutheran theologians I have checked primary sources where possible. Three major compendia have been of help: Heinrich L. Heppe, *Reformed Dogmatics*, tr. by G. T. Thomson (London: George Allen & Unwin, Ltd., 1950); Heinrich F. Schmid, *The Doctrinal Theology of the Evangelical Lutheran Church*, tr. by Charles A. Hay and Henry E. Jacobs (3d ed.; Augsburg Publishing House, 1961); M. Schneckenberger, *Vergleichende Darstellung des lutherischen und reformierten Lehrbegiffs* (Stuttgart: J. B. Metzlerschen, 1855), 2 vols.

2. Brian A. Gerrish, "Atonement and 'Saving Faith,' " *Theology Today*, Vol. XVII, No. 2 (July, 1960), pp. 181–191.

3. John Calvin, *Institutes of the Christian Religion*, II. xii. 4.

4. Amandus Polanus à Polandorf, *Syntagma theologiae Christianae*, VI. 27., quoted from Heppe, *op. cit.*, p. 448.

5. Johannes Wollebius, *Compendium theologiae Christianae*, ed. by E. Bizer (Neukirchen, 1935), XVIII. xxiii. Prop. I. For a similar position among the Lutherans, see J. A. Quenstedt, *Theologico didactio polemica* (1685).

6. David Hollazius, *Examen theologicum acromaticum* (n.p., 1707), p. 737.

7. Wollebius, *op. cit.*, p. 12.

8. Calvin, *op. cit.*, I. xiii. 21.

9. "Liberalism," *The Catholic Encyclopedia*, ed. by Haberman and Pace (Robert Appleton Co., 1914), Vol. 9., p. 212.

10. Jacques Maritain, *Three Reformers* (Charles Scribner's Sons, 1950), p. 4.

11. *Ibid.*, p. 19.

12. *Ibid.*, p. 168.

13. Gotthold Ephraim Lessing, "Anti-Goeze I," *Sämtliche Schriften,* ed. by Lachmann (Leipzig: G. I. Goeschen'sche, 1856), Vol. 10, p. 151.

14. Albrecht Ritschl, *The Christian Doctrine of Justification and Reconciliation,* tr. by H. R. Mackintosh and A. B. Macaulay (2d ed.; Edinburgh: T. & T. Clark, 1902), pp. 391 ff.

15. *Ibid.,* p. 394.

16. Wilhelm Niesel, *The Theology of Calvin,* tr. by Harold Knight (The Westminster Press, 1956), pp. 22–29 and 54–58.

17. Edward A. Dowey, Jr., *The Knowledge of God in Calvin's Theology* (Columbia University Press, 1952), pp. 3–40.

18. Calvin, *Institutes,* IV. viii. 9; III. viii. 12; I. xvii. 2; *et al.*

## Chapter II. Pioneers of a New Way

1. Sebastian Castellio, *De arte dubitandi,* II. ii., quoted from a book of texts ed. by Heinold Fast, *Der linke Flügel der Reformation* (Bremen: Carl Schueneman Verlag, 1962), p. 384.

2. Desiderius Erasmus, *The Enchiridion,* tr. by Raymond Himelick (Indiana University Press, 1963), Ch. 14, The Fifth Rule, p. 112.

3. Martin Chemnitz, *Loci theologici* (Francofurti and Wittebergae, 1653), Locus VII, p. 201.

4. *Ibid.,* p. 197.

5. *Ibid.*

6. Erasmus, *The Enchiridion,* Ch. 3, p. 47.

7. *Ibid.,* Ch. 6, p. 58.

8. *Ibid.,* Ch. 6, p. 70

9. *Ibid.,* Ch. 12, The Third Rule, p. 93.

10. *Ibid.,* Ch. 1, p. 37.

11. Desiderius Erasmus, *Paraclesis,* text from *Desiderius Erasmus Roterdamus: Ausgewählte Werke,* ed. by H. Holborn (Munich: Beck, 1933), p. 142.

12. Michael Servetus, *On the Errors of the Trinity,* tr. by Earl Morse Wilbur (Harvard University Press, 1932), Bk. I, p. 6.

13. *Ibid.,* I. 60, p. 67.

14. *Ibid.,* I. 30, p. 34.

15. *Ibid.,* I. 1, p. 6.

16. *Ibid.,* VII. 14, p. 183.

17. *Ibid.,* IV, Synopsis, p. 131.

18. *Catechism of the Churches of Poland, which confess, according to Scripture, one God the Father* . . . , III. 1., pp. 34–35. I had the opportunity of consulting a 1659 edition of the catechism made in Amsterdam (Irenopolis). The book and chapter headings are standard. The page references are to an English translation by Thomas Rees (London: Longman, Hurst, Rees, Orem and Brown, 1818), which is the only generally available source of the text in the United States.

19. *Ibid.*

20. *Ibid.,* V. 8., p. 311.

21. Robert South, "Jesus of Nazareth Proved the True and Only Promised Messiah," a sermon found in a book of texts, *Anglicanism,* ed. by Paul E. More and Frank L. Cross (London: S.P.C.K., 1935), p. 86.

22. The spread of Socinianism in the English-speaking world is traced by H. John McLachlan, *Socinianism in Seventeenth-Century England* (London: Oxford University Press, 1951).

## Chapter III. CHRIST AND THE NEW WORLD OF MAN

1. Not only is there internal evidence of Socinianism in Locke's writings but there is convincing external evidence of Locke's knowledge of Socinianism. See McLachlan, *op. cit.*, pp. 325–327.

2. Richard Hooker, *The Laws of Ecclesiastical Polity*, Bk. 2, Sec. 3 (London: Holdsworth & Bell, 1830), Vol. I, p. 183.

3. William Laud, *A Relation of the Conference Between William Laud and Mr. Fisher the Jesuit*, from Laud's *Works* (Oxford: John Henry Parker Society, 1849), Vol. II, p. 89.

4. Francis Cheynell, *The Rise, Growth and Danger of Socinianism* (London: 1643), p. 40.

5. Edward, Lord Herbert of Cherbury, *De Veritate*, tr. by Meyrick H. Carre (Bristol: University of Bristol, 1937), p. 121.

6. *Ibid.*, pp. 289–307.

7. *Ibid.*, p. 307.

8. *Ibid.*, p. 312.

9. *Ibid.*, p. 75.

10. Quoted from the annotations to the *Principia* made by Florian Cajori. Sir Isaac Newton, *Mathematical Principles*, tr. by Andrew Mott, rev. by Florian Cajori (University of California Press, 1960), p. 669.

11. Sir Isaac Newton, *Opticks* (4th ed.; Whittlesey House, McGraw-Hill Book Company, Inc., 1931), p. 405.

12. *Ibid.*, p. 402.

13. *Ibid.* Also see Newton, *Principia* (Mathematical Principles), pp. 528–542.

14. Newton, *Principia*, p. 544.

15. Newton, *Opticks*, p. 370.

16. Newton, *Principia*, p. 545.

17. *Ibid.*, p. 398.

18. Edwin A. Burtt, *The Metaphysical Foundations of Modern Physical Science* (rev. ed.; Doubleday & Company, Inc., 1954), p. 284.

19. Baruch Spinoza, *Theologico-Political Treatise*, Ch. VI.

20. Christoph Wittich, *Anti-Spinoza* (Amstelaedami, 1690) and *Theologia pasifica defensa* (Amstelaedami, 1689).

## Chapter IV. JESUS THE MESSIAH

1. John Locke, *The Reasonableness of Christianity, Works* (11th ed.; London: W. Otridge *et al.*, 1812), Vol. VII, p. 106.

2. John Locke, *An Essay Concerning Human Understanding*, ed. by A. S. Pringle-Pattison (Oxford: At the Clarendon Press, 1924), IV. 9. 3.

3. *Ibid.*, IV. 10. 6.

4. Locke, *The Reasonableness of Christianity*, p. 6.

5. *Ibid.*, p. 139.

6. *Ibid.*, p. 144.

7. *Ibid.*, p. 33.

8. *Ibid.*, p. 85.

9. *Ibid.*, p. 120.

10. *Ibid.*, p. 11.

11. *Ibid.*, p. 14.

12. *Ibid.*, p. 105.

13. *Ibid.*, p. 11.

14. *Ibid.*, p. 149.

15. John Edwards, *Socinianism Unmask'd* (London, 1696), pp. 17–18.

16. *Ibid.*, p. 60.

17. John Edwards, *Some Thoughts Concerning the Several Causes and Occasions of Atheism Especially in the Present Age* (London, 1695), p. 110.

18. Edwards, *Socinianism Unmask'd*, p. 78.

19. Locke, *The Reasonableness of Christianity*, p. 106.

20. Edwards, *Socinianism Unmask'd*, p. 81.

21. Laud, *op. cit.*, pp. 121–122.

22. Locke, *The Reasonableness of Christianity*, p. 135.

23. John Locke, A *Discourse on Miracles*, found in a collection of Locke's religious writings ed. by Ian T. Ramsey (London: Adam and Charles Black, Ltd., 1958), p. 79.

24. *Ibid.*, p. 84.

25. Samuel Clarke, *The Scripture Doctrine of the Trinity* (2d ed.; London, 1719), p. ii.

26. Stephen Nye, *A Second Collection of Tracts, Proving the God and Father of Our Lord Jesus Christ, the only True God* . . . (n.p., 1693), p. 17.

27. *Ibid.*, p. 12.

28. *Ibid.*, p. 5.

29. Clarke, *op. cit.*, p. vii.

30. *Ibid.*, p. viii.

31. *Ibid.*, p. 73.

32. *Ibid.*, p. 237.

33. *Ibid.*, p. 263.

34. *Ibid.*, p. 162.

35. This is documented by William B. Hunter, Jr., "Milton's Arianism Reconsidered," *Harvard Theological Review*, 52 (1959), pp. 9–35, and "Some Problems in John Milton's Theological Vocabulary," *Harvard Theological Review*, 57 (1964), pp. 353–365.

36. Henrici à Diest, *Theologia Biblica* (Deventer, 1643), par. 208, quoted by Heppe, *op. cit.*, p. 488.

## Chapter V. DEISM, DOUBT, AND HISTORY

1. John Toland, *Christianity Not Mysterious* (2d ed.; London, 1702), p. 172.

2. *Ibid.*

3. *Ibid.*, p. 24.

4. *Ibid.,* p. 38.

5. *Ibid.,* p. 49.

6. *Ibid.,* p. 53.

7. *Ibid.,* p. 145.

8. John Toland, *Nazarenus: Jewish, Gentile and Mahometan Christianity* (2d ed.; London: J. Brotherton, J. Roberts, and A. Dodd, 1718).

9. Thomas Woolston, *A Discourse on the Miracles of Our Saviour* (3d ed.; London: Thomas Woolston, 1727), p. 14.

10. Anthony Collins, *The Scheme of Literal Prophecy Considered* (London, 1727), p. 327.

11. Woolston, *op. cit.,* pp. 10 and 18.

12. Collins, *The Scheme of Literal Prophecy Considered,* p. 335.

13. Anthony Collins, *A Discourse on the Grounds and Reasons of the Christian Religion* (London, 1724), p. 40.

14. Matthew Tindal, *Christianity as Old as the Creation, or the Gospel a Republication of the Religion of Nature* (Newburgh: David Dennison, 1798), p. 241.

15. *Ibid.,* p. 75.

16. *Ibid.,* p. 47.

17. *Ibid.,* p. 19.

18. *Ibid.,* p. 27.

19. David Hume, *An Enquiry Concerning Human Understanding,* ed. by L. A. Selby-Bigge (Oxford: At the Clarendon Press, 1892), X. I., p. 88.

20. *Ibid.*

21. *Ibid.,* X. I. 87.

22. *Ibid.,* X. I. 90.

23. *Ibid.,* X. I. 91.

24. *Ibid.,* X. II. 92–93.

25. *Ibid.,* X. II. 98.

26. *Ibid.,* X. II. 100.

27. *Ibid.,* X. II. 101.

28. Quoted from McLachlan, *op. cit.,* p. 338.

### Chapter VI. PIETY, PHILOSOPHY, AND CHRIST

1. Gottfried Wilhelm von Leibniz, *Theodicy,* Preliminary Dissertation I, 1, from *G. W. Leibniz Philosophische Werke,* ed. by Kirchmann (Leipzig: Verlag von Felix Meiner, 1904), Vol. IV, p. 33.

2. Gottfried Wilhelm von Leibniz, *Monadology and Other Philosophical Essays,* tr. and ed. by Paul Schrecker (Liberal Arts Press, Inc., The Bobbs-Merrill Company, Inc., 1965), p. 13.

3. Leopold Zscharnack, *Lessing und Semler* (Gressen: Alfred Töpelmann, 1905), pp. 25–26.

4. Gottfried Arnold, *Aus der Theologia Experimentalis,* par. 5. Text of this and other texts on Pietism are in *Das Zeitalter des Pietismus,* ed. by Schmidt and Jannasch (Bremen: Carl Schuenemann Verlag, 1955), p. 164.

5. Philipp Jakob Spener, *Von der Wiedergeburt,* par. 3, from Schmidt and Jannasch, *op. cit.,* p. 57.

6. Zscharnack, *op. cit.*, pp. 19–24.

7. Johann Albrecht Bengel, *Versuch einer apokalyptischen Zeittafel*, found in Schmidt and Jannasch, *op. cit.*, pp. 201–204.

8. Albert Schweitzer, *The Quest of the Historical Jesus*, tr. by W. Montgomery (The Macmillan Company, 1961), p. 27.

9. Emanuel Hirsch, *Geschichte der neuern evangelischen Theologie* (Gütersloh: Verlagshaus Gerd Mohn, 1949), Vol. IV, p. 9.

10. *Ibid.*, p. 59.

11. Johann Salomo Semler, *Letztes Glaubensbekenntniss über natürliche und christliche Religion* (Königsberg, 1792), p. 176.

12. Johann Salomo Semler, *Abhandlung von freiern Untersuchung des Canon* (Halle, 1771–1775), Vol. I, p. 75.

13. Semler, *Letztes Glaubensbekenntniss*, p. 187.

14. *Ibid.*, p. 69.

15. *Ibid.*, p. 214.

16. *Ibid.*, p. 216.

17. Hirsch, *op. cit.*, p. 52.

18. Semler, *Letztes Glaubensbekenntniss*, pp. 245–246.

19. *Ibid.*

20. *Ibid.*, p. 239.

21. *Ibid.*, p. 345.

22. *Ibid.*, p. 220.

23. Johann Salomo Semler, *Versuch einer freiern theologischen Lehrart, zur Bestätigung und Erläuterung seines lateinischen Buchs* (Halle in Magdeburgischen, 1777), p. 455.

24. Semler, *Versuch*, p. 450.

25. Semler, *Letztes Glaubensbekenntniss*, p. 215.

26. *Ibid.*

27. Semler, *Versuch*, p. 450.

28. Semler, *Letztes Glaubensbekenntniss*, p. 120.

29. Semler, *Versuch*, p. 455.

30. *Ibid.*, p. 450.

31. *Ibid.*, p. 465.

## Chapter VII. ALL THE WAY WITH REASON

1. Heinrich P. K. Henke, *Lineamenta institutionum fidei Christianae historicocriticarum*, quoted from Hirsch, *op. cit.*, Vol. IV, p. 11.

2. Heinrich E. G. Paulus, *Das Leben Jesu, als Grundlage einer reinen Geschichte des Urchristentums* (Heidelberg: D. F. Winter, 1828), Vol. II, Part I, p. 3.

3. *Ibid.*, Vol. II, Part 1, p. 424.

4. *Ibid.*, Vol. II, Part 1, p. 81.

5. Hugh J. Schonfield, *The Passover Plot* (London: Hutchinson & Co., Publishers, Ltd., 1965), p. 132.

6. Paulus, *op. cit.*, Vol. II, Part 1, pp. 2–3.

7. *Ibid.*, Vol. I, Part 1, p. xv.

8. The version of the Lord's Prayer by Sintenis is from Luther D. Reed, *The Lutheran Liturgy* (Muhlenberg Press, 1947), pp. 147–148.

9. David Friedrich Strauss, *Das Leben Jesu* (4th ed.), Sec. 147.

### Chapter VIII. THE QUESTION OF FUNDAMENTALS

1. Edward Gibbon, *The Decline and Fall of the Roman Empire,* ed. by D. M. Low (Washington Square Press, 1962), Vol. I, p. 182.
2. *Ibid.,* p. 398.
3. Leonardus Riisenius, *Francisi Turretini Compendium Theologiae,* XI. 39. 4.
4. Gotthold Ephraim Lessing (ed.), *Von dem Zwecke Jesu und seiner Jünger. Nach ein Fragment des Wolfenbüttelschen Ungenannten* (Braunschweig, 1778), pp. 27–28.
5. *Ibid.,* p. 23.
6. *Ibid.,* p. 153.
7. *Ibid.,* p. 126.
8. Schweitzer, *op. cit.,* p. 24.
9. Lessing, *Sämtliche Schriften,* Vol. 10, p. 38.
10. Joseph Butler, *Works,* ed. by W. E. Gladstone (Oxford: At the Clarendon Press, 1897), Vol. I, p. 89.
11. David Hume, *An Enquiry Concerning Human Understanding,* X.1 and XI.
12. David Hume, *Essays Moral, Political and Literary,* ed. by T. H. Green and T. H. Grose (London: Longmans, Green & Co., Ltd., 1875), Vol. I, p. 220.
13. David Hume, *Dialogues Concerning Natural Religion,* ed. by Norman K. Smith (Oxford: At the Clarendon Press, 1935), Part XII, p. 281.
14. Hume, *Enquiry,* XII. III., p. 164.
15. Immanuel Kant, *Critique of Pure Reason,* ed. by J. M. D. Meiklejohn (rev. ed.; Wiley Book Company, Inc., 1943), III. IV., p. 336.
16. *Ibid.,* II. III., p. 269.

### Chapter IX. THE END AND THE BEGINNING

1. Hume, *Dialogues,* Part XII, p. 281. The term "religious hypothesis" and the material on the relation of religion to the good of society comes from the *Enquiry,* Sec. XI, and from the *Natural History,* Chs. IX to XII.
2. Hume, *Dialogues,* Part XII, p. 281. Smith in his Introduction to the *Dialogues* demonstrates textually that this whole section was a later addition by Hume to soften the offense of his critique of theology.
3. Quoted from Hirsch, *op. cit.,* Vol. V, p. 124.
4. Ernst W. Hengstenberg, *Christology of the Old Testament,* tr. by Theodore Meyer and James Martin from the 2d German ed. of 1857 (Kregel Publications, 1956), Vol. IV, p. 323.
5. *Ibid.,* p. 233.
6. *Ibid.,* p. 326.
7. C. C. J. Webb, *Kant's Philosophy of Religion* (Oxford: Oxford University Press, 1926), p. 12.
8. Immanuel Kant, *Religion Within the Limits of Reason Alone,* tr. by Theodore M. Greene and Hoyt H. Hudson (Harper & Row, Publishers, Inc., 1960), p. 100.

9. Immanuel Kant, *Critique of Practical Reason*, tr. by Abbott (6th ed.; London: Longmans, Green & Co., Ltd., 1909), I. I. II., p. 145.

10. *Ibid.*, II. II. I., p. 210.

11. *Ibid.*, II. II. VI., p. 231.

12. Kant, *Religion*, pp. 5–6.

13. *Ibid.*, p. 122.

14. *Ibid.*, p. 101.

15. *Ibid.*, p. 32.

16. *Ibid.*, p. 42.

17. *Ibid.*, p. 73.

18. *Ibid.*, p. 136.

19. *Ibid.*, pp. 54–55.

20. *Ibid.*, p. 56.

21. *Ibid.*, p. 110.

22. *Ibid.*, p. 68.

23. *Ibid.*, p. 69.

# INDEX